MINCED BEEF COOKBOOK

CW01583170

MINCED BEEF COOKBOOK

Carole Cooper

LONDON
W FOULSHAM & CO LTD
New York Toronto Cape Town Sydney

W Foulsham & Co Ltd
Yeovil Road, Slough, Berks, England

ISBN 0-572-00950-X

© Copyright W Foulsham & Co Ltd 1977

Designed by Peter Constable
Cover picture by courtesy of M.E.A.T.
Printed in Hong Kong

CONTENTS

METRICATION

It is very important to use either the imperial table for measuring ingredients *or* the metric one, and not to mix them when preparing a recipe. The metric scale is not an exact translation of the imperial one, which would be very cumbersome, but the recipes have been tested to arrive at the correct proportions. The metric result is approximately 10% less than that gained with imperial measurements. The metric scale recommended for British use allows 25 g to 1 oz; and 25 ml to 1 fl oz, instead of the true scale of 28 g to 1 oz. This means that quantities must be 'rounded up' at certain points on the scale, or else vital amounts will be lost as total recipe quantities become larger.

Solid Measures

½ oz	15 g
1 oz	25 g
2 oz	50 g
3 oz	75 g
4 oz	100 g
5 oz	125 g
6 oz	150 g
7 oz	175 g
8 oz	225 g
9 oz	250 g
10 oz	300 g
11 oz	325 g
12 oz	350 g
13 oz	375 g
14 oz	400 g
15 oz	425 g
16 oz	450 g or 500 g
1½ lb	750 g
2 lb	1 kg

Liquid Measures

½ fl oz	15 ml
1 fl oz	25 ml
2 fl oz	50 ml
3 fl oz	75 ml
4 fl oz	100 ml
¼ pint	125 ml
⅓ pint	175 ml
½ pint	250 ml
⅔ pint	350 ml
¾ pint	375 ml
1 pint	500 ml
1¼ pints	625 ml
1½ pints	750 ml
1¾—2 pints	1 litre

When meat and vegetables and some groceries are purchased in metric measure, they will normally be in 1 lb or 2 lb measurement equivalents, and people will ask for .5 kg or 1 kg which is 500 g or 1000 g. When baking, a measurement of 450 g is in proportion with the smaller amounts of ingredients needed.

INTRODUCTION

Mince is one of the most versatile ingredients in our kitchens, and we have always considered it to be nutritious, but hardly exciting. Perhaps this is because we have lacked imagination in the use of such a basic food. Today, younger cooks are more aware of the value of tasty herbs, spices and vegetables, and we can use all these to make mince more interesting and suitable for a wide variety of meals.

With the busy housewife in mind, I have compiled this book, taking into consideration not only family meals and simple snacks, but more elaborate recipes which are suitable for impressing the boss or the grandest guests.

I trust that you will find as much enjoyment in these pages as I have had in writing the recipes.

Carole Cooper

Chapter One

ALL ABOUT MINCE

There is an art in buying and cooking mince, and a good dish starts in the butcher's shop. When buying mince, you can choose the quality you want, though you may have to pay more for it. Often the ready-minced beef on display consists of odd meat trimmings with a lot of fat, and when this is cooked the mince is hard and greasy and a lot of fat is released. For perfect cooking, choose the lean cut of meat in the piece and mince it yourself or ask the butcher to mince it specially for you. A good chuck steak is ideal for mince dishes, or rump for something special. If you want to use lamb for a dish (and many of these recipes can be used with lamb instead of beef), choose shoulder lamb for mincing.

Correct seasoning is the second secret of preparing delicious mince dishes. Season with sea salt and freshly milled black pepper, and always taste and re-season if necessary before serving. Keep a supply of good fresh curry powder and other ground spices, some concentrated tomato purée in a can or tube, and some beef or other flavoured stock cubes. Herbs are essential for cookery with a flavour. If dried ones are used, they are twice as strong as the fresh variety. It is a good idea to buy dried herbs in only small quantities as they begin to taste musty very quickly. Garlic is another flavour enhancer. Garlic salt may be used, but then the salt in the recipe should be adjusted accordingly. Garlic cloves give the best flavour, which is released by crushing the garlic with a flat-bladed knife and a little coarse salt to aid crushing.

For the best flavour and texture, mince should be

sealed in a little fat before simmering gently in the liquid in the recipe. If mince is not sealed first, the flavour will be watery and the colour poor; slow cooking ensures a smooth soft texture without hard lumps.

Quantities

The recipes in this book are designed for 4–6 people, according to appetite. With mince recipes, servings may be easily extended with potatoes, bread, grilled tomatoes, or an extra vegetable, so an unexpected guest need never feel left out.

Metrication

For recipes, the Metrication Board has recommended a scale of 25 g to 1 oz, and 25 ml to 1 fl.oz, and the recipes in this book are scaled accordingly. Meat and vegetables are traditionally bought in 1 lb and 2 lb quantities, and there is a little adjustment in these larger amounts to give the correct proportion in recipes e.g. 1 lb meat is usually quoted in recipes as .5 kg (for shopping purposes), or as 450 g where the correct proportion of ingredients is more critical, although with 25 g to 1 oz, this would be 400 g to 1 lb. In meat cookery, the proportion of ingredients is not usually so critical as in the preparation of cakes and puddings where a dish can be easily ruined if there is an incorrect proportion of solids to liquids.

Chapter Two

MINCE EXTENDERS

A number of meal-stretchers are on the market made from soya protein, which helps to produce cheaper meals, but old habits die hard, and it will probably be a long time until full use is made of them. Vegetable protein is much cheaper to produce than animal protein, with one acre annually producing 500 lb soya, 180 lb wheat but only 60 lb beef, and soya beans are the richest known natural source of protein. From habit, people like meat and do not take naturally to a bean diet which is acceptable to some vegetarians, so that manufacturers have had to make considerable efforts to make vegetable protein more tempting to the public in general.

The beans are processed by extrusion or spinning to produce dry pieces in chunks or granules, now known as TSP (textured soya protein), but formerly called TVP (textured vegetable protein). Extruded TSP is cheaper, but the spinning process gives a better quality, and this type of TSP may be used as a complete substitute for meat. Soya protein compares favourably with meat protein as it provides most of the essential amino acids, but it also contains almost no fat or cholesterol and only half the calorific value of fresh meat.

Soya protein may be bought in dry form or as a canned meal. The dry variety has to be reconstituted with water according to manufacturer's instructions, and usually takes up two or three times its dry weight. Dry soya protein will keep up to eighteen months dry, but once it has been mixed with liquid, it should be treated as fresh meat, stored in a refrigerator and used up quickly. Soya protein may be unflavoured, or have added flavouring and colouring. The unflavoured varieties may be used with appropriate flavourings to produce 'ham', 'pork' or 'beef' dishes. While soya protein may be used to produce complete dishes, it is generally more acceptable to the family mixed with beef, usually in a proportion of one-third soya protein to two-thirds beef mince. The money saved by using such a proportion of soya protein is only a few pence in a dish, but there is no nutritional loss and the flavour can be just as good. Meat-extenders can be purchased at supermarkets and grocers, in health food shops, and in some butchers.

Chapter Three

QUICK AND EASY

There is nothing like a little minced beef to make quick, tasty and nourishing snacks. Small quantities of cooked mince can be used for small pies or for stuffing vegetables, or for adding bulk to egg or cheese dishes. Although these dishes make quick snacks, they can be used as a complete main course with the addition of vegetables or a salad, potatoes or crusty French bread.

Hot Stuffed Tomatoes

	Imperial	*Metric*	*American*
Tomatoes	*4*	*4*	*4*
Cooked minced meat	*4 oz*	*100 g*	*¾ cup*
Hard-boiled eggs	*1*	*1*	*1*
Sage and onion stuffing	*2 oz*	*50 g*	*½ cup*

Cut the tomatoes in half. Remove the centres and put tomatoes on a greased baking tin. Mix the minced meat and chopped hard-boiled egg together with the stuffing. Sieve the tomato centres and mix with the beef and put into the tomato cases. Bake at 350°F/180°C/Gas Mark 4 for 20 minutes.

Cold Stuffed Tomatoes

Large tomatoes	*4*	*4*	*4*
Hard-boiled eggs	*1*	*1*	*1*
Cooked mince	*4 oz*	*100 g*	*¾ cup*
Mayonnaise			
Cucumber and lettuce for decoration			

Remove the tops of the tomatoes, scoop out the tomato centres and mix with chopped egg, and the mince. Pile into the tomato shells. Top with thick mayonnaise and serve on a bed of lettuce and cucumber.

Quick Beef Patties

	Imperial	Metric	American
Raw minced beef	*1 lb*	*450 g*	*2 cups*
Onion, medium size	*1*	*1*	*1*
Egg	*1*	*1*	*1*
Breadcrumbs	*2 oz*	*50 g*	*½ cup*
Pinch of mixed herbs			
Salt and pepper			
Butter, melted	*2 oz*	*50 g*	*¼ cup*
Tomatoes	*2*	*2*	*2*

Blend the minced beef with chopped onion, seasoning, breadcrumbs, egg and herbs. Form into 4 round cakes. Brush with the butter and grill or fry until golden brown for 5–10 minutes. Garnish with grilled tomato halves.

Very Quick Spaghetti Bolognese

	Imperial	Metric	American
Minced beef	*1 lb*	*450 g*	*2 cups*
Packet mixed vegetable soup			
Water	*1 pint*	*500 ml*	*2½ cups*

Put beef, packet soup and water into a pan and bring to the boil. Stir until boiling, then simmer gently for 20 minutes. Season to taste. Serve over cooked spaghetti.

Minced Beef Potato Nests

	Imperial	Metric	American
Mashed potatoes	*1 lb*	*450 g*	*1 lb*
Cooked minced beef	*6 oz*	*150 g*	*1⅛ cup*
Butter, melted	*2 oz*	*50 g*	*¼ cup*

Pipe the potatoes into nest shapes. Fill with the minced beef. Brush with melted butter. Bake at 400°F/200°C/Gas Mark 6 for 15 minutes.

Italian Beef Club Sandwiches

	Imperial	Metric	American
Cooked minced beef	*4 oz*	*100 g*	*3/4 cup*
Dash of Tabasco sauce			
Pepper, chopped	*1/2*	*1/2*	*1/2*
Tomato	*1*	*1*	*1*

Mix beef, Tabasco and chopped pepper. Take 6 slices of bread, toast then spread the mixture on the first two slices and sandwich together. Place tomato slices on top of sandwiches and serve at once.

Egg Ramekins

	Imperial	Metric	American
Cooked minced beef	*4 oz*	*100 g*	*3/4 cup*
White sauce	*1/2 pint*	*250 ml*	*1 1/4 cups*
Salt and pepper			
Eggs	*4*	*4*	*4*
Butter			

Mix beef with the white sauce. Season to taste. Lightly butter 4 individual ramekins. Put mixture into the bottom of each dish and break in eggs. Dot with butter and bake at 375°F/190°C/Gas Mark 5 for 12 minutes until set.

Vol-au-Vents

	Imperial	Metric	American
Vol-au-vents cases	*6*	*6*	*6*
Cooked minced beef	*4 oz*	*100 g*	*3/4 cup*

Defrost the vol-au-vent cases, bake and fill with hot mince. Serve immediately.

Variations

(a) Mushrooms, chopped	*2 oz*	*50 g*	*5/8 cup*
(b) Bacon, chopped rashers	*4*	*4*	*4*
(c) Cheese, grated	*2 oz*	*50 g*	*3/4 cup*
(d) Peppers, chopped	*2 oz*	*50 g*	*1/2 cup*

Hungry Man's Sandwich

	Imperial	*Metric*	*American*
Slices of bread	*6*	*6*	*6*
Cooked minced beef	*4 oz*	*100 g*	*3/4 cup*
Mushrooms, cooked, chopped	*2 oz*	*50 g*	*5/8 cup*
Bacon, cooked, chopped rashers	*5-6*	*5-6*	*5-6*

Toast 6 slices of bread to make two sandwiches. Spread beef on one slice, mushroom and bacon on the second. Top with third slice and serve immediately.

Quick Beef Fritters

	Imperial	*Metric*	*American*
Egg	*1*	*1*	*1*
Milk	*1/4 pint*	*125 ml*	*5/8 cup*
Flour, sieved	*2 oz*	*50 g*	*1/2 cup*
Beef stock cube, crumbled	*1*	*1*	*1*
Minced beef	*12 oz*	*300 g*	*1 1/2 cups*
Onion, grated	*1*	*1*	*1*
Mixed herbs	*1/2 tsp*	*1/2 tsp*	*1/2 tsp*

Mix the egg and milk into the flour. Add the beef cube, minced beef, herbs and onion and mix well. Leave for 30 minutes. Fry spoonfuls of mixture for 5 minutes on each side.

Savoury Beef Puffs

	Imperial	*Metric*	*American*
Margarine	*12 oz*	*300 g*	*1½ cups*
Flour	*1 lb*	*450 g*	*4 cups*
Pinch of salt			
Water			
Cooked minced beef	*8 oz*	*200 g*	*1½ cups*

Rub fat, flour and salt together until they resemble fine breadcrumbs. Mix with cold water to a workable dough. Divide mixture in two and roll out thinly. Mark pastry into 2 in. squares and place $1\frac{1}{2}$ teaspoonfuls of mince on one half of each piece of pastry. Fold over and press sides well down. Fry in shallow fat until golden. Serve on cocktail sticks. These may be served with a tossed salad or with pre-dinner drinks.

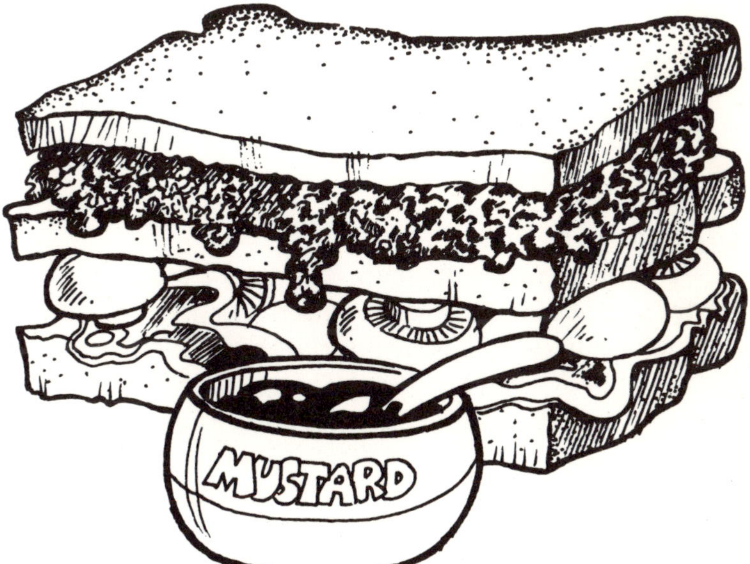

Chapter Four

COUNTRY STYLE

Country people have always known the value of minced meat to feed their hungry families. By the ingenious use of pastry, potatoes and root vegetables, they have stretched a small quantity of beef or lamb to make filling and nourishing main courses.

Potato and Beef Roll

	Imperial	Metric	American
Raw minced beef	*1 lb*	*450 g*	*2 cups*
Fat bacon	*4 oz*	*100 g*	*¼ lb*
Potatoes, cooked	*4*	*4*	*4*
Chutney	*2 tbsp*	*2 tbsp*	*2 tbsp*
Salt and pepper			
Egg	*1*	*1*	*1*
A little flour			
Parley to garnish			

Mix beef, minced bacon, diced potatoes and chutney and season well. Bind with the beaten egg, and form into a roll, using a little flour to shape. Grease a strip of kitchen foil to wrap around the roll to hold its shape as the mixture is soft, and then wrap in more foil and put on a baking tray. Cook at 350°F/180°C/Gas Mark 4 for 1 hour, and then unroll. Cut into 4 pieces, lift carefully on to a dish and garnish with parsley. Serve with gravy or hot tomato sauce.

Beef Plate Pie

	Imperial	Metric	American
Shortcrust pastry	6 oz	150 g	6 oz
Cooked minced beef	6 oz	150 g	1⅛ cups
Prepared mustard	1 tsp	1 tsp	1 tsp
Tomatoes	2	2	2
Salt and pepper			
Pinch of mixed herbs			
Chutney	1 tbsp	1 tbsp	1 tbsp

Divide pastry into two, and roll out each piece large enough to fit an 8 in. flan ring. Grease the inside of the flan ring, stand it on a well-greased baking tin and line with one round of the rolled dough. Trim off excess pastry. Mix all remaining ingredients together for filling including sliced tomatoes. Cover the pastry with this and top with remaining piece of pastry. Brush with a little beaten egg or milk. Bake at 400°F/200°C/Gas Mark 6 for 30 minutes.

Stuffed Baked Marrow

	Imperial	Metric	American
Onions	2	2	2
Cooked minced beef	12 oz	300 g	2¼ cups
Breadcrumbs	4 oz	100 g	1 cup
Pinch of sage			
Salt and pepper			
Marrow or winter squash, medium size	1	1	1
Dripping	2 oz	50 g	¼ cup

Chop the onions and fry them lightly. Mix the minced beef, onions, breadcrumbs, sage, salt and pepper together. Cut the end off the marrow, peel and scoop out the centre. (If it is a very young marrow the peel can be left on.) Fill the marrow with the mixture and replace the cut end securing with a skewer. Heat the dripping in a meat tin, put in the marrow and baste with the fat. Bake at 400°F/200°C/Gas Mark 6 for 1 hour. Serve cut in slices with gravy.

Savoury Meat Squares

	Imperial	Metric	American
Flour	*4 oz*	*100 g*	*1 cup*
Salt and pepper			
Cooking fat	*3 oz*	*75 g*	*3/8 cup*
Mashed potatoes	*4 oz*	*100 g*	*1 cup*
A little cold water			
Beaten egg or milk to glaze			

Filling

	Imperial	Metric	American
Large onion	*1*	*1*	*1*
Large tomatoes	*2*	*2*	*2*
Cooking fat	*1 oz*	*25 g*	*1/8 cup*
Raw minced beef	*8 oz*	*200 g*	*1 cup*

To make the pastry, add salt and pepper to flour, and rub in the cooking fat. Add the potatoes, and knead firmly, adding enough water to give a firm dough. To make the filling, chop the onion and tomatoes. Fry in hot fat until soft. Remove from the fat and cook the minced beef for 20 minutes. Add the cooked onion and tomatoes. Roll out the pastry into two oblongs. Spread the filling over one and cover with the other. Seal the edges with water, score the top and brush with a little egg or milk. Bake at 425°F/220°C/Gas Mark 5 for 40 minutes. Cut in squares to serve with gravy.

Serve with carrots or a green vegetable.

Crispy Mince Bake

	Imperial	Metric	American
Onion, medium size	*1*	*1*	*1*
Raw minced beef	*12 oz*	*300 g*	*1½ cups*
Parsley, chopped	*1 tbsp*	*1 tbsp*	*1 tbsp*
Gravy browning	*½ oz*	*12 g*	*1 tbsp*
Salt and pepper			
Beans in tomato sauce, small can	*1*	*1*	*1*
Bread slices, large	*6*	*6*	*6*
Butter	*1 oz*	*25 g*	*⅛ cup*
Yeast extract	*1 tsp*	*1 tsp*	*1 tsp*
Eggs	*2*	*2*	*2*

Peel and chop the onion. Place minced beef and onion in a saucepan to which parsley has been added and cook over a moderate heat, stirring occasionally, for 15 minutes. Stir in gravy browning, salt and pepper, beans and ½ pint/250 ml water. Bring to the boil, stirring, then cover and simmer for 15 minutes. Pour into a shallow ovenware dish. Make three rounds of sandwiches with the bread, butter and yeast extract. Cut off the crusts with a sharp knife. Butter the top of each sandwich and cut each into four triangles. Dip each triangle into beaten egg. Arrange, buttered side up, on the mince. Bake at 350°F/180°C/Gas Mark 4 for 20 minutes until the bread is golden brown and crisp.

Serve hot with peas or beans.

Mince in the Hole

	Imperial	Metric	American
Lard	1 oz	25 g	1/8 cup
Raw minced beef	8 oz	200 g	1 cup
Fresh white breadcrumbs	1 oz	25 g	1/4 cup
Tomato puree	3 tbsp	3 tbsp	3 tbsp
Salt and pepper			
Eggs	2	2	2
Onion, medium size	1	1	1
Flour	4 oz	100 g	1 cup
Pinch of salt			
Milk	1/2 pint	250 g	1 1/4 cups
Gouda cheese, grated	4 oz	100 g	1 1/2 cups

Melt the lard in a roasting tin and place in the oven at 425°F/220°C/Gas Mark 7. Mix thoroughly the mince, breadcrumbs, tomato purée, salt and pepper. Bind with 1 beaten egg. Shape the mixture into 10 balls and place in the hot fat in the baking tin. Cover with slices of onion and return to the oven for 10 minutes. Put sifted flour and salt into a bowl, gradually beat in the second egg with the milk. Mix well until smooth. Pour the batter into the tin around the meatballs and return to the oven at 450°F/230°C/Gas Mark 8 for 30 minutes, until well risen and golden. Sprinkle with grated cheese and return to the oven for 5 minutes. Serve immediately, with green salad or a green vegetable.

Minced Beef Crumble

	Imperial	Metric	American
Raw minced beef	12 oz	300 g	1½ cups
Onion, chopped	3 oz	75 g	¾ cup
Flour	4 oz	100 g	1 cup
Tomato puree	1 tbsp	1 tbsp	1 tbsp
Stock	½ pint	250 ml	1¼ cups
Salt and pepper			
Butter	2 oz	50 g	¼ cup
Cheddar cheese, grated	2 oz	50 g	¾ cup
Mixed herbs	2 tsp	2 tsp	2 tsp
Chopped parsley			

Cook the mince and chopped onion until meat is brown. Add half the flour, tomato purée, stock, salt, pepper and herbs. Place in an ovenware dish. Rub butter into the remaining flour until it resembles fine breadcrumbs. Stir in grated cheese and spoon over the mixture. Bake at 375°F/190°C/Gas Mark 5 for 50 minutes. Sprinkle with chopped parsley before serving.

Serve hot with plenty of creamy mashed potatoes, and green beans.
Drink an Italian red wine or lager or cider.
Follow with stewed fruit or with a fruit water ice, or with fresh fruit if preferred.

Friday Pie

	Imperial	Metric	American
Potatoes	*2 lb*	*1 kg*	*2 lb*
Butter	*1 oz*	*25 g*	*1/8 cup*
Milk	*3 tbsp*	*3 tbsp*	*3 tbsp*
Salt and pepper			
Lard	*1 oz*	*25 g*	*1/8 cup*
Onion, chopped	*4 oz*	*100 g*	*1 cup*
Raw minced beef	*1 lb*	*450 g*	*2 cups*
Flour	*1/2 oz*	*12 g*	*2 tbsp*
Stock	*1/4 pint*	*125 ml*	*5/8 cup*
Tomato	*1*	*1*	*1*
Mixed vegetables, canned or frozen	*5 oz*	*125 g*	*1 heaped cup*

Boil the potatoes, cream them with butter and milk and season to taste. Melt the lard in frying pan and fry the chopped onion until golden brown. Add minced beef and cook gently for 5 minutes. Season, add flour and mix well. Stir in the stock and bring to the boil. Reduce the heat and simmer for 5 minutes. Mix the mince with the vegetables and place in an ovenware casserole. Arrange the sliced tomato on top. Pipe creamed potatoes on top to cover, or spoon on and mark with a fork. Bake at 375°F/190°C/Gas Mark 5 for 30 minutes until golden brown.

Serve hot with a green vegetable, and with some additional fried potatoes.
Drink beer or cider.
Follow with a fruit pie baked in the same oven, or with treacle tart.

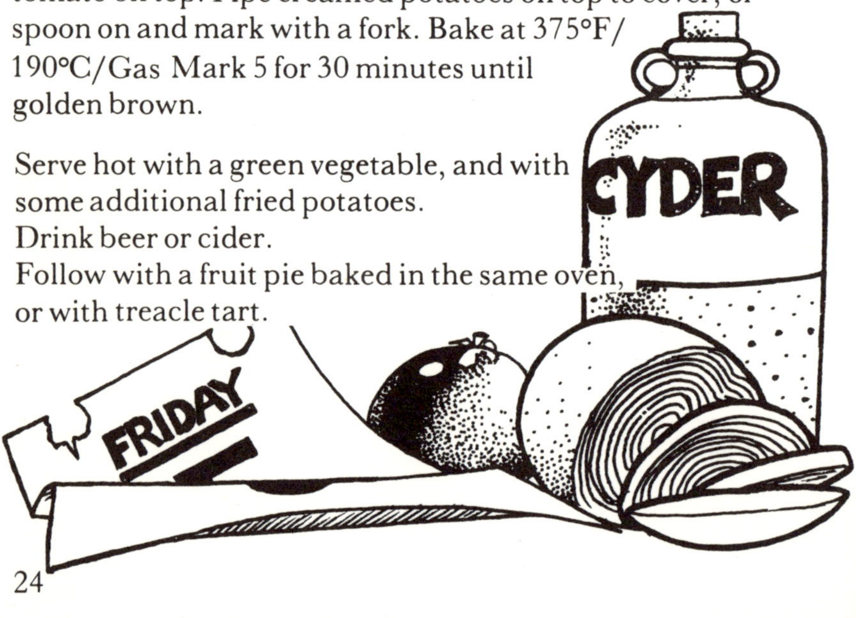

Beef and Potato Pasties

	Imperial	*Metric*	*American*
Oil	*1 tbsp*	*1 tbsp*	*1 tbsp*
Potatoes	*8 oz*	*200 g*	*½ lb*
Carrot	*1*	*1*	*1*
Onion, small	*1*	*1*	*1*
Raw minced beef	*12 oz*	*300 g*	*1½ cups*
Beef stock cube	*1*	*1*	*1*
Salt and pepper			
Puff pastry	*12 oz*	*300 g*	*¾ lb*
Milk to glaze			

Dice the potatoes, carrot and onion and gently fry in a frying pan with the oil for 3–4 minutes. Lift out, using a draining spoon. Fry the meat quickly to seal, then add the potato, onion, carrot, crumbled stock cube, salt and pepper. Leave to cool. Roll out pastry thinly and cut out four 7 in./18 cm rounds using a plate as a guide. Divide the filling between the rounds, brush edges with milk, bring the pastry up and seal on top by pressing together with fingertips. Place pasties on a baking sheet, brush over with milk to glaze. Bake at 425°F/220°C/Gas Mark 7 for 15 minutes then reduce the heat to 350°F/180°C/Gas Mark 4 for a further 25 minutes.

Serve hot with a green vegetable and gravy.

Cornish Mince Pasties

	Imperial	*Metric*	*American*
Flour	*1 lb*	*450 g*	*4 cups*
Salt	*1 tsp*	*1 tsp*	*1 tsp*
Lard	*6 oz*	*150 g*	*3/4 cup*
Suet	*2 oz*	*50 g*	*1/4 cup*
Water to mix			
Filling			
Potatoes, large	*2*	*2*	*2*
Turnip, small	*1*	*1*	*1*
Onion	*1*	*1*	*1*
Salt and pepper			
Minced beef	*12 oz*	*300 g*	*1½ cups*
Chopped parsley	*1 tsp*	*1 tsp*	*1 tsp*

Mix the flour and salt, rub in the lard and add the suet. Mix to a stiff paste with water and roll out to $\frac{1}{4}$ in./.75 cm thickness. Cut into rounds using a small plate to cut to size. Slice potatoes, turnip and onion finely and place mixture on centre of each round, seasoning well. Place mince and parsley on top. Damp edges of each round and close pastry across top, sealing the edges firmly with water. Pinch edges between finger and thumb to give fluted tops. Put on a baking sheet and bake at 450°F/230°C/Gas Mark 8 for 10 minutes. Reduce heat to 350°F/180°C/Gas Mark 4 and cook until meat is tender, which will take about 45 minutes.

Serve hot with vegetables, or cold with salad.

Two Crust Pie

	Imperial	*Metric*	*American*
Onion, small	*1*	*1*	*1*
Mushrooms, sliced	*2 oz*	*50 g*	*5/8 cup*
Fat	*2 oz*	*50 g*	*1/4 cup*
Curry powder	*1 tsp*	*1 tsp*	*1 tsp*
Parsley, chopped	*1 tsp*	*1 tsp*	*1 tsp*
Raw minced beef	*1 lb*	*450 g*	*2 cups*
Mixed vegetables, cooked or frozen	*2 oz*	*50 g*	*1/2 cup*
Gravy	*1/4 pint*	*125 ml*	*5/8 cup*
Shortcrust pastry	*6 oz*	*150 g*	*6 oz*
Salt and pepper			
Egg or milk to glaze			

Fry chopped onion and sliced mushrooms until soft. Stir in curry powder and parsley and cook for 3 minutes. Add meat and vegetables and cook through. Add gravy and seasoning. Roll out half the pastry, line an 8 in./20 cm pie dish and fill with mixture. Roll remaining half of the pastry and make a pie lid. Place over the filling and seal edges well with water. Glaze pie with egg or milk. Bake at 400°F/200°C/Gas Mark 6 for 30 minutes. Reduce heat to 350°F/180°C/Gas Mark 4 and continue baking for 20 minutes.

Serve hot with peas, beans or a green vegetable.
Serve cold with a green salad or mixed salad.
Drink red wine, beer or cider.
Follow with fresh fruit and cheese, or ice cream.

Scottish Beef Roll

	Imperial	*Metric*	*American*
Onion, small	*1*	*1*	*1*
Streaky bacon	*8 oz*	*200 g*	*½ lb*
Raw minced beef	*1 lb*	*450 g*	*2 cups*
Carrot, large	*1*	*1*	*1*
Porridge oats	*4 oz*	*100 g*	*1⅓ cups*
Worcestershire sauce	*1 tbsp*	*1 tbsp*	*1 tbsp*
Salt and pepper			
Pinch of mixed herbs			
Egg	*1*	*1*	*1*
Browned breadcrumbs			

Grease a large piece of foil. Peel the onion and chop finely. Put in mixing bowl with minced beef. Remove rind from bacon, cut bacon into small pieces and add to the minced beef. Peel the carrot and grate into the mixture. Add the oats, Worcestershire sauce, salt and pepper, and herbs. Beat egg in a basin; mix well and add to the meat mixture blending well. Turn the mixture out on to prepared foil and form into a roll about 6 in./15 cm long. Wrap well. Place roll on a baking sheet and bake at 300°F/150°C/Gas Mark 2 for 2 hours. Leave to cool for 15 minutes, then unwrap carefully. Press browned breadcrumbs all over roll. Leave until completely cold, then cover beef roll loosely with foil and chill in the refrigerator.

To serve cold: cut beef roll into thick slices and serve with various salads or pickles.

To serve hot: cut beef roll into thick slices; grill or fry for about 5 minutes on each side until brown. Serve with hot vegetables, or in buttered rolls for a quick snack dish.

Spiced Herb Balls in Sauce

	Imperial	*Metric*	*American*
Sage and onion stuffiing	*2 oz*	*50 g*	*½ cup*
Mixed herbs	*1 tsp*	*1 tsp*	*1 tsp*
Egg	*1*	*1*	*1*
Raw minced beef	*12 oz*	*300 g*	*1½ cups*
Salt and pepper			
Beef extract cube	*1*	*1*	*1*
Flour	*1 oz*	*25 g*	*¼ cup*
Oil	*2 tbsp*	*2 tbsp*	*2 tbsp*

Sauce

Onion, medium	*1*	*1*	*1*
Curry powder	*1 tbsp*	*1 tbsp*	*1 tbsp*
Mustard powder	*2 tsp*	*2 tsp*	*2 tsp*
Dark soft brown sugar	*1 oz*	*25 g*	*⅛ cup*
Cornflour	*½ oz*	*12 g*	*⅛ cup*
Vinegar	*2 tsp*	*2 tsp*	*2 tsp*
Worcestershire sauce	*2 tsp*	*2 tsp*	*2 tsp*

Mix the sage and onion stuffing with herbs with 4 tablespoons/60 ml boiling water in a bowl and leave for 5 minutes. Add the beaten egg to the minced beef and add salt and pepper to taste. Crumble extract cube into flour on a plate. Form the meat mixture into 16 even-sized balls and roll each one in the flour. Heat the oil in a large frying pan, and fry the meatballs until browned. Drain and place in a medium-sized saucepan. Peel the onion, slice finely and add with the curry powder to the oil left in the frying pan. Fry for 10 minutes, adding more oil if necessary. Add mustard, sugar, cornflour, vinegar and Worcestershire sauce. Add ¾ pint/375 ml/1⅞ cups water and bring to the boil, stirring continuously. Lower the heat and cook for 2 minutes. Pour the sauce over the meatballs in the saucepan. Bring to the boil, and simmer for 50 minutes. Serve with creamy mashed potatoes.

Baked Beef Dumplings

	Imperial	*Metric*	*American*
Mixed root vegetables (carrots, onions, turnips, swedes or parsnips)	*2 lb*	*1 kg*	*2 lb*
Celery sticks	*3*	*3*	*3*
Oil	*3 tbsp*	*3 tbsp*	*3 tbsp*
Flour	*1 oz*	*25 g*	*¼ cup*
Salt and pepper			
Tomato purée	*1 tsp*	*1 tsp*	*1 tsp*
Yeast extract	*2 tsp*	*2 tsp*	*2 tsp*
Boiling water			
Raw minced beef	*12 oz*	*300 g*	*1½ cups*
Pinch of mixed dried herbs			
Self-raising flour or flour sifted with 2 tsp baking powder	*7 oz*	*175 g*	*1¾ cups*
Suet, shredded	*3 oz*	*75 g*	*⅜ cup*
Salt	*1 tsp*	*1 tsp*	*1 tsp*

Prepare the vegetables by slicing the carrots and onions and cutting the turnips, swede or parsnips into small cubes. Scrub the celery and cut into slices. In a large saucepan heat the oil and fry the vegetables gently, stirring occasionally, for 15 minutes. Add the flour, salt and pepper. Dissolve the tomato purée, and yeast extract in 1 pint/500 ml/2½cups boiling water, add to the saucepan and bring to the boil. Pour into a shallow casserole, cover with a lid and place in the centre of the oven. Place the minced beef in a bowl. Add the herbs and pepper to taste and blend well. Turn out on to a floured board and form into a roll; cut into 6 even-sized pieces. Roll each piece into a ball with floured hands and then coat each in flour. Heat an extra 2 tablespoons/30 ml oil in a frying pan. Fry the meatballs gently until browned and drain on kitchen paper. Mix flour, suet and salt in a bowl. Add 6 tablespoons/90 ml water and mix with a fork to form a soft, but not sticky dough. Turn out on to a floured board and divide into 6 pieces. Roll out this dough in circles. Place a meatball in the centre of each piece and mould the pastry around it to cover it completely. Place the dumplings on a baking tray and bake at 375°F/190°C/Gas Mark 5 for 30 minutes, along with the casserole of vegetables. Serve dumplings hot with the root vegetables. Cook jacket potatoes in the oven for the hungry ones.

Beefy Potatoes

	Imperial	*Metric*	*American*
Potatoes, very large	*4*	*4*	*4*
Butter	*2 oz*	*50 g*	*¼ cup*
Cooked minced beef	*3 oz*	*75 g*	*⅝ cup*
Tomato	*1*	*1*	*1*
Parsley to garnish			

Scrub potatoes, prick with a fork and bake at 350°F/180°C/Gas Mark 4 for 1½ hours. Halve the potatoes, scoop out the pulp, and mix it with butter and beef. Return to the potato cases, decorate with sliced tomato and return to oven to re-heat. Garnish with sprigs of parsley before serving.

Serve with broccoli or cabbage, or serve a green salad to follow.

Drink red wine or beer.

Follow with a baked milk pudding, such as rice or tapioca, accompanied by a spoonful of marmalade and some thick cream on each portion.

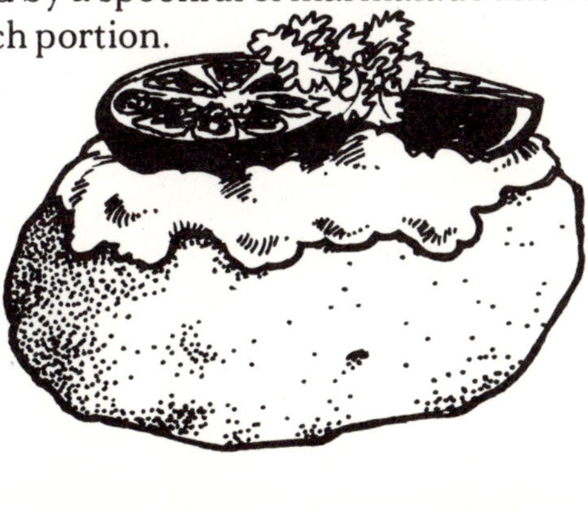

Savoury Surprise

	Imperial	*Metric*	*American*
Cheddar cheese, grated	*2 oz*	*50 g*	*¾ cup*
Streaky bacon rashers	*4*	*4*	*4*
Raw minced beef	*8 oz*	*200 g*	*1 cup*
Pinch of mixed dried herbs			
Salt and pepper			
Flour	*½ oz*	*12 g*	*2 tbsp*
Beef extract cube	*1*	*1*	*1*
Potato, large	*1*	*1*	*1*
Puff pastry	*12 oz*	*300 g*	*¾ lb*
Egg or milk to glaze			

Grate the cheese. Remove the rind from the bacon and cut it into small pieces. Place bacon, minced beef, herbs, salt, pepper and flour into a bowl. Crumble the beef extract cube and add to meat mixture. Prepare and dice the potato and add to the bowl, mixing well. Roll out the pastry and trim to an oblong, 12 × 9 in./30 × 23 cm. Brush both long edges with milk. Turn the pastry so that the short sides are at the side. With the back of a knife, mark 2 lines, one 3½ in./8 cm. and one 2½ in./6 cm. in from edge of each side. Cut ½ in./1 cm. wide strips slanting from edge on each side up to lines marked 2½ in./6 cm. in. Place the filling within the marked centre panel and sprinkle with cheese. Place pastry strips alternately from each side over filling to form a plait. Seal ends by pressing pastry down firmly. Lift on to a baking sheet, and brush with egg or milk to glaze. Bake at 400°F/200°C/Gas Mark 6 for 30 minutes. Reduce heat to 325°F/170°C/Gas Mark 3 and cook for a further 25 minutes. Serve hot or cold.

Creamed Mince

	Imperial	Metric	American
Onion, large	*1*	*1*	*1*
Carrot, large	*1*	*1*	*1*
Celery sticks	*2*	*2*	*2*
Oil	*2 tbsp*	*2 tbsp*	*2 tbsp*
Minced beef	*1 lb*	*450 g*	*2 cups*
Salt and pepper			
Pinch of sage			
Milk	*¼ pint*	*125 ml*	*⅝ cup*
Vinegar	*2 tsp*	*2 tsp*	*2 tsp*
Condensed mushroom soup, medium can	*1*	*1*	*1*
Ribbon noodles	*8 oz*	*200 g*	*½ lb*
Butter	*½ oz*	*12 g*	*1 tbsp*
Parsley			

Peel and finely slice the onion. Scrub the celery and carrot and slice finely. Heat oil in a large saucepan. Add the vegetables and cook for about 6 minutes on low heat. Add the minced beef, salt, pepper and sage. Cook slowly, stirring continuously until browned. Add milk, vinegar and soup, and bring to the boil, stirring. Reduce the heat, cover and cook slowly for 30 minutes. Cook noodles in boiling, salted water for 10 minutes. Drain in a colander and rinse with hot water. Return to the pan, add butter and toss until the noodles are well coated. Pile the noodles on to a warmed serving dish. Taste and add more salt and pepper to meat mixture if necessary. Pile meat on top of noodles, and decorate with a sprig of parsley.

Minced Beef Splits

	Imperial	*Metric*	*American*
Butter	*1 oz*	*25 g*	*1/8 cup*
Onion	*1*	*1*	*1*
Oil	*1 tbsp*	*1 tbsp*	*1 tbsp*
Minced beef	*1 lb*	*450 g*	*2 cups*
Beef stock cube	*1*	*1*	*1*
Condensed beef soup, medium can	*1*	*1*	*1*
Worcestershire sauce	*1 tsp*	*1 tsp*	*1 tsp*
Tomato Purée	*3 tbsp*	*3 tbsp*	*3 tbsp*
Soft finger rolls	*4*	*4*	*4*
Vinegar	*3 tbsp*	*3 tbsp*	*3 tbsp*
Soft brown sugar	*1 tsp*	*1 tsp*	*1 tsp*
Frankfurters	*4*	*4*	*4*

Melt butter and lightly fry the chopped onion in a frying pan. Drain the onion and reserve. Heat oil in a pan and quickly brown the mince. Stir in 4 tablespoons/60 ml soup, the crumbled stock cube, Worcestershire sauce and half the tomato purée. Cut the rolls lengthwise and toast lightly. Place rolls on a baking sheet. Spoon mince on to them to cover and put a split frankfurter into each. Bake at 450°F/230°C/Gas Mark 8 for 10 minutes. Meanwhile, heat together the remaining soup, tomato purée, vinegar and sugar. Serve sauce over splits with a little fried onion on each.

A side salad can be served with these.

Fake Steak

	Imperial	*Metric*	*American*
Minced beef	*2 lb*	*1 kg*	*4 cups*
Tomato ketchup	*2 tbsp*	*2 tbsp*	*2 tbsp*
Parsley, chopped	*½ tbsp*	*½ tbsp*	*½ tbsp*
Nutmeg, grated			
Salt and pepper			
Pinch of mixed herbs			
Eggs	*2*	*2*	*2*
Onion	*1*	*1*	*1*
Flour			
Butter or oil for frying			

Mix the minced beef with tomato ketchup, parsley, nutmeg, salt, pepper and herbs. Separate 1 egg and keep the white aside. Beat the yolk with the other whole egg and use to bind the meat mixture. Divide into portions and shape to resemble steaks. Dredge with flour on all sides. Fry in heated butter or oil on both sides until well browned. Then drain and keep hot. Peel and slice the onion. Coat with flour, dip into the beaten egg white, then into flour again and fry until golden and crisp. Garnish the meat with the onion slices.

Serve with chips and peas, or with a green salad or tomato salad.
Drink red wine, beer or cider.
Follow with a steamed pudding or with fruit fritters.

Hamburgers

	Imperial	Metric	American
Raw minced beef	*1 lb*	*450 kg*	*2 cups*
Onion, small	*1*	*1*	*1*
Salt and pepper			
Melted butter or oil for coating			
or *a little fat for shallow cooking*			

Mix the minced beef and chopped onion with salt and pepper. Shape lightly into 8 round flat cakes. Brush with the butter or oil and grill for 5 minutes, or fry in a little fat, turning once. Hamburgers can be served rare or well done. Traditionally they contain no other ingredients but can be varied by adding one of the following to the basic mixture:

(a) Cheese, grated	*3 oz*	*75 g*	*1⅛ cups*
(b) Pickle	*1 tbsp*	*1 tbsp*	*1 tbsp*
(c) Prepared mustard	*2 tsp*	*2 tsp*	*2 tsp*
(d) Mixed herbs	*1 tsp*	*1 tsp*	*1 tsp*
(e) Chopped parsley	*1 tbsp*	*1 tbsp*	*1 tbsp*
(f) Mushrooms, sliced	*2 oz*	*50 g*	*⅝ cup*
(g) Tomatoes, chopped and skinned			

Serve with chips, peas, tomatoes and mushrooms, or in split toasted soft rolls.
Serve with beer or a cup of coffee.
Follow with a slice of fruit tart, or with fresh fruit and cheese.

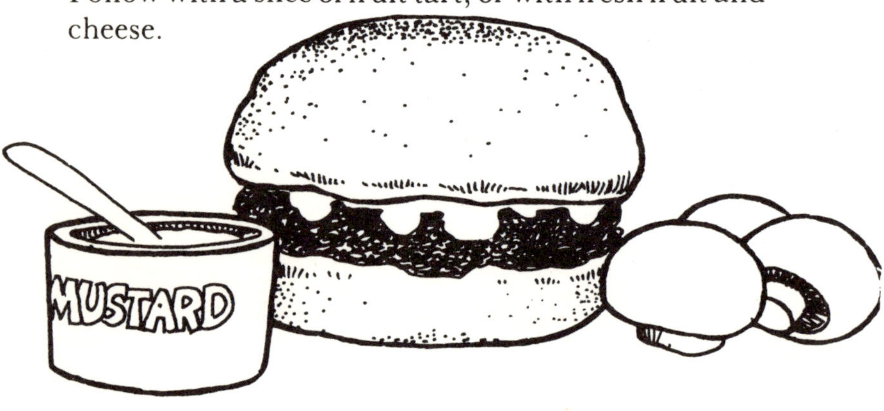

Pepper Mill Hamburgers

	Imperial	Metric	American
Onion, medium	*1*	*1*	*1*
Salt and pepper			
Raw minced beef	*1 lb*	*450 g*	*2 cups*
Black pepper	*1 tbsp*	*1 tbsp*	*1 tbsp*
Butter	*1 oz*	*25 g*	*⅛ cup*
Oil	*1 tbsp*	*1 tbsp*	*1 tbsp*
Dry red wine	*¼ pint*	*125 ml*	*⅝ cup*
Beef stock cube	*1*	*1*	*1*

Chop up the onion, add salt and pepper and knead it into the minced beef. Form into four round shapes and sprinkle both sides of each with coarse ground pepper. Press the pepper well in to each round. Heat butter and oil in a heavy frying pan and fry the hamburgers gently for 10 minutes turning once. Pour the red wine over them, and loosen the pan drippings with a wooden spoon. Bring to the boil. Reduce the heat and simmer for a few minutes. Remove the meat with a draining spoon and keep them hot. Stir crumbled stock cube into wine juices and simmer until reduced by half. Serve meat with the wine sauce. Freshly ground black peppers are essential for this recipe, and nothing else will taste the same.

Serve with creamy mashed potatoes and broccoli.
Drink red wine, or cider.
Follow with a bowl of sugared fruit and cream, or with ice cream gâteau.

Minced Beef Croquettes

	Imperial	*Metric*	*American*
Butter or margarine	*1 oz*	*25 g*	*1/8 cup*
Flour	*1 oz*	*25 g*	*1/4 cup*
Milk	*1/4 pint*	*125 ml*	*5/8 cup*
Mixed herbs	*2 tsp*	*2 tsp*	*2 tsp*
Gherkins, chopped	*2 tsp*	*2 tsp*	*2 tsp*
Cooked minced beef	*12 oz*	*300 g*	*2 1/4 cups*
Soft white breadcrumbs	*3 oz*	*75 g*	*3/4 cup*
Salt and pepper			
Egg	*1*	*1*	*1*
Crisp breadcrumbs	*2 oz*	*50 g*	*1/2 cup*
Lard or oil for frying			

Make a thick sauce of butter or margarine, flour and milk. Add mixed herbs, gherkins and the mince, mix well, then stir in breadcrumbs, salt and pepper. Let mixture cool and form into eight finger shapes. Brush with beaten egg and coat with crisp breadcrumbs. Fry in hot fat until crisp and brown and drain well on absorbent paper. Serve hot or cold.

Serve hot with boiled potatoes, beans or a green vegetable.
Serve cold with a green salad, beetroot or tomato salad.
Drink beer or cider.
Follow with treacle tart or fruit crumble.

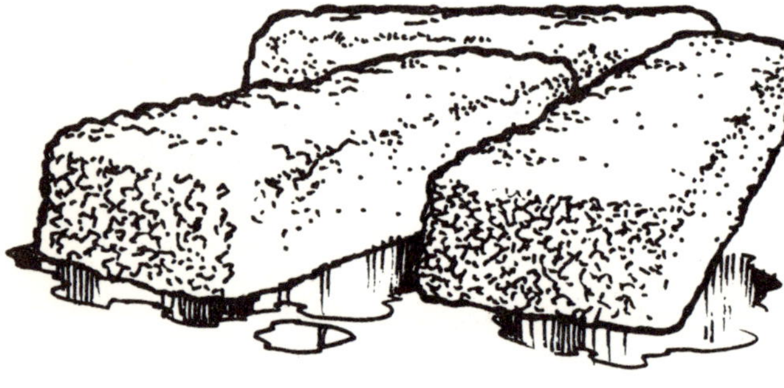

Beef and Corn Puffs

	Imperial	*Metric*	*American*
Flour	*4 oz*	*125 g*	*1 cup*
Pinch of salt			
Egg	*1*	*1*	*1*
Milk	*¼ pint*	*125 ml*	*⅝ cup*
Cooked minced beef	*4 oz*	*100 g*	*¾ cup*
Can sweetcorn kernels, small	*1*	*1*	*1*
Fat for deep frying			
Parsley sprigs			

Sift the flour and salt into a mixing bowl. Make a well in the centre and add the egg yolk. Beat gently, adding the milk gradually, until all the flour is mixed in, then beat well for about 2 minutes. Leave the batter to stand in a cool place until needed. Add the mince and the drained sweetcorn to the batter just before cooking. Whisk the egg white stiffly and fold evenly into the batter. Fry spoonfuls of the mixture in hot deep fat for 3 minutes until crisp and golden. Serve immediately, decorated with parsley.

Serve with peas and carrots.
Drink beer or cider.
Follow with stewed fruit or a fruit water ice.

Creole Minced Beef

	Imperial	*Metric*	*American*
Corn oil	*1 tbsp*	*1 tbsp*	*1 tbsp*
Onion, large	*1*	*1*	*1*
Raw minced beef	*1½ lb*	*675 g*	*3 cups*
Salt and pepper			
Pinch of nutmeg			
Beef stock cube	*1*	*1*	*1*
Raisins	*2 oz*	*50 g*	*½ cup*
Water	*¾ pint*	*375 ml*	*1⅞ cups*
Cornflour	*½ oz*	*12 g*	*⅛ cup*
Triangles of toast for garnish			
Hard-boiled eggs	*2*	*2*	*2*
Chives, chopped			

Heat the oil and cook the mince and chopped onion until brown. Add salt and pepper, nutmeg, raisins and beef stock cube. Stir in water, bring to the boil and simmer until meat is tender. Add cornflour with a little water. Stir into the beef and bring to the boil, stirring all the time. Cook for 3 minutes. Place the beef in a hot dish. Arrange triangles of toast around the edge, and decorate with chopped egg and chives mixed together.

Serve with boiled rice, and follow with a green salad.
Drink beer or cider.
Follow with fresh or stewed fruit.

Creole Cottage Pie

	Imperial	Metric	American
Onion, medium	*1*	*1*	*1*
Margarine	*2 oz*	*50 g*	*¼ cup*
Raw minced beef	*1 lb*	*450 g*	*2 cups*
Flour	*1 oz*	*25 g*	*¼ cup*
Chicken stock	*¼ pint*	*125 ml*	*⅝ cup*
Tomato puree	*2 tbsp*	*2 tbsp*	*2 tbsp*
Sherry	*2 tsp*	*2 tsp*	*2 tsp*
Pinch of curry powder			
Tarragon	*1 tsp*	*1 tsp*	*1 tsp*
Salt and pepper			
Potatoes, peeled	*1½ lb*	*675 g*	*1½ lb*
Milk	*1 tbsp*	*1 tbsp*	*1 tbsp*
Egg yolk	*1*	*1*	*1*

Fry the chopped onion in margarine until golden brown and remove from the pan. Cook the beef, stirring until the meat is well browned. Add the onion and flour, the stock, tomato purée and sherry. Add the curry powder and tarragon and season to taste. Mix the ingredients well and then transfer to a casserole with lid. Cook at 350°F/180°C/Gas Mark 4 for 30 minutes. While the meat is cooking, boil the potatoes, drain, mash with a little margarine, milk, egg yolk and seasoning. Spread the potatoes over the meat and put back in the oven without lid until golden brown, which will take about 25 minutes.

Serve with a green vegetable or peas.

Pepper Beef

	Imperial	Metric	American
Cooking oil			
Red pepper	*1*	*1*	*1*
Green pepper	*1*	*1*	*1*
Tomatoes, large	*3*	*3*	*3*
Onion	*1*	*1*	*1*
Raw minced beef	*4 oz*	*100 g*	*½ cup*
Salt and pepper			
Potatoes	*2 lb*	*1 kg*	*2 lb*

Heat the oil and fry the chopped peppers, sliced tomatoes and onion for about 15 minutes until cooked. Remove from pan and cook beef for 20 minutes. Boil the potatoes, drain and put into a hot casserole dish. Add the pepper mixture to the cooked meat, season well, and heat for 5 minutes. Pour the mixture over the potatoes.

Nutty Beef Stew

	Imperial	Metric	American
Raw minced beef	*1½ lb*	*675 g*	*3 cups*
Canned tomatoes	*14 oz*	*350 g*	*1¾ cups*
Beef stock	*¾ pint*	*375 ml*	*1⅞ cups*
Onion, small	*4*	*4*	*4*
Salt and pepper			
Crunchy peanut butter	*2 tbsp*	*2 tbsp*	*2 tbsp*
A little flour to thicken			
Mixed nuts	*1 oz*	*25 g*	*¼ cup*

Put beef in a pan and fry gently. Drain off the fat. Add the tomatoes and their juices, whole onions, stock, salt and pepper. Simmer for 1 hour, stirring occasionally. Add peanut butter and stir well. Simmer for 10 minutes. Thicken with flour if necessary. Add mixed nuts just before serving and serve with boiled rice.

Beef Pancakes

	Imperial	*Metric*	*American*
Pancakes, made from ½ pint/250 ml/⅝ cup of batter	*8*	*8*	*8*
Butter	*4 oz*	*100 g*	*½ cup*
Onion, large	*1*	*1*	*1*
Carrots	*2*	*2*	*2*
Raw minced beef	*1½ lb*	*675 g*	*3 cups*
White wine	*6 oz*	*150 ml*	*¾ cup*
Tomato puree	*2 tbsp*	*2 tbsp*	*2 tbsp*
Beef stock	*1 pint*	*500 ml*	*2½ cups*
Salt and pepper			
Pinch of nutmeg			
Egg yolks	*3*	*3*	*3*
Parmesan cheese, grated	*6 oz*	*150 g*	*2¼ cups*
White sauce	*½ pint*	*250 ml*	*1¼ cups*
Parsley to garnish			

Make the pancakes and set aside. Melt the butter in large saucepan, add chopped onion and grated carrot and cook for 10 minutes until browned. Add meat and cook, stirring, for a further 20 minutes. Add wine, tomato purée, stock, salt and pepper. Cook for 3 hours. Remove from the heat and allow to cool. Add nutmeg, egg yolks and half the cheese and mix to a paste. Place two tablespoons in centre of each pancake. Roll up and place in a shallow greased dish. Pour the sauce over and sprinkle with remaining cheese. Bake at 400°F/200°C/Gas Mark 6 for 10 minutes. Garnish with parsley and serve.

Shepherd's Pie Shells

	Imperial	Metric	American
Minced cooked beef	8 oz	200 g	1½ cups
Onion, medium	1	1	1
Salt and pepper			
Pinch of tarragon			
Rich brown sauce	¼ pint	125 ml	⅝ cup
Mashed potatoes	1 lb	450 g	4 cups
Tomato	1	1	1
Parsley, chopped	1 tsp	1 tsp	1 tsp

Grease 4 scallop shells. Mix the minced meat, chopped fried onion, seasoning and tarragon with enough sauce to make a dropping consistency. Divide the mixture between the 4 shells. Surround the meat with a border of mashed potato and cover the meat with a tomato slice. Bake at 400°F/200°C/Gas Mark 5 for 10 minutes and slightly brown the potatoes. Serve hot, garnished with parsley.

Beef and Liver Loaf

	Imperial	Metric	American
Lamb's liver	8 oz	200 g	½ lb
Raw minced beef	1 lb	450 g	2 cups
Onion, small	1	1	1
Bacon rashers	2	2	2
Soft white breadcrumbs	3 oz	75 g	2 cups
Salt and pepper			
Mixed herbs	1 tsp	1 tsp	1 tsp
Egg	1	1	1

Soak the liver in cold water for 30 minutes, then remove skin and tough veins and mince the liver finely. Add liver to the minced beef and finely minced onion, minced bacon and breadcrumbs. Season to taste, add herbs and bind with the beaten egg. Pack lightly in a loaf tin, cover with kitchen foil and bake at 350°F/180°C/Gas Mark 4 for 1 hour. Serve cold.

Minced Beef Parcel

	Imperial	Metric	American
Carrot	1	1	1
Mushrooms, chopped	1 oz	25 g	1/4 cup
Onion	1	1	1
Raw minced beef	12 oz	300 g	1 1/2 cups
Lard	1/2 oz	12 g	1 tbsp
Peas	1 oz	25 g	1/8 cup
Flour	1 oz	25 g	1/4 cup
Beef stock	1/4 pint	125 ml	5/8 cup
Shortcrust pastry	12 oz	300 g	3/4 lb

Chop the carrot, mushrooms and onion. Cook the mince, carrot and onion until the meat is brown. Add the peas and mushrooms. Stir in the flour with stock and bring to the boil. Simmer for 10 minutes. Cool the mixture and place in centre of 12 in. square of pastry. Fold in corners and make a parcel. Bake at 400°F/200°C/Gas Mark 6 for 30 minutes.

Lamb and Red Kidney Bean Casserole

	Imperial	Metric	American
Minced shoulder lamb	1 lb	450 g	2 cups
Button onions	8 oz	200 g	1/2 lb
Red kidney beans, large can	1	1	1
Tomatoes, large can	1	1	1
Cayenne pepper	2 tsp	2 tsp	2 tsp
Stock	1/2 pint	250 ml	1 1/4 cups
Salt and pepper			

Brown the meat in its own fat. Add the peeled onions and fry gently for 10 minutes. Add the remaining ingredients. Cover and simmer for 1 hour. Before serving, check the seasoning and thicken with a little cornflour dissolved in cold water if necessary.

Beef and Pork Loaf

	Imperial	*Metric*	*American*
Raw minced beef	*8 oz*	*200 g*	*1 cup*
Raw minced pork	*8 oz*	*200 g*	*1 cup*
Pork sausage meat	*8 oz*	*200 g*	*½ lb*
Soft white breadcrumbs	*8 oz*	*200 g*	*5⅓ cups*
Parsley, chopped	*2 tbsp*	*2 tbsp*	*2 tbsp*
Eggs	*2*	*2*	*2*
Tomato purée	*2 tbsp*	*2 tbsp*	*2 tbsp*
Salt	*1 tsp*	*1 tsp*	*1 tsp*
Black pepper	*1 tsp*	*1 tsp*	*1 tsp*
Garlic clove	*½–1*	*½–1*	*½–1*

Mix all the ingredients until well blended. Spread the mixture evenly in a loaf tin and cover with kitchen foil. Place the tin in a roasting pan and pour water into the roasting pan to depth of 1 in./2½ cm. Cook just below the centre of the oven at 325°F/170°C/Gas Mark 3 for 2½ hours. Allow to cool, turn out on to a plate and place in the refrigerator to chill. Serve with a green salad.

Serve hot with gravy, or tomato or mushroom sauce, and vegetables.
Serve cold with salad, or sliced in sandwiches.
Drink lager or cider.
Follow with a milk pudding baked in the same oven.

Beef Decker

	Imperial	*Metric*	*American*
Onion, large	*1*	*1*	*1*
Garlic clove	*½–1*	*½–1*	*½–1*
Salt			
Oil	*2 tbsp*	*2 tbsp*	*2 tbsp*
Raw minced beef	*1 lb*	*450 g*	*2 cups*
Flour	*1½ oz*	*40 g*	*¼ cup+ 2 tbsp*
Worcestershire sauce	*2 tsp*	*2 tsp*	*2 tsp*
Egg	*1*	*1*	*1*
Evaporated milk, small can	*1*	*1*	*1*
Cheddar cheese, grated	*4 oz*	*100 g*	*1½ cups*
Mashed potato			

Line the base and sides of a loose-bottomed 6 in./15 cm deep cake tin with a large piece of foil. Press into base and up the side, bringing foil up over the top. Peel the onion and slice thinly. Crush the garlic. Heat the oil in a frying pan. Add onion and garlic, and fry over a low heat for about 10 minutes until soft. Drain. Put meat, flour, Worcestershire sauce, egg, evaporated milk and a pinch of salt in a bowl. Beat well. Place a third of the meat mixture in the prepared tin and level the surface. Place onion on top of meat mixture. Add another third of meat mixture on top and sprinkle with half the grated cheese. Put remaining meat mixture on top and sprinkle with remaining cheese. Bring foil up to cover the top Place on a baking sheet and bake at 350°F/180°C/Gas Mark 4 for 40 minutes. Open foil and bake for a further 20 minutes until top is brown. Leave in tin for 10 minutes. Remove from tin and remove the foil. Place on an ovenware plate, pour juices over and keep warm. Pipe some mashed potatoes round the Beef Decker and return to the oven until the potato is browned. Serve cut in wedges.

Saucy Meat Balls

	Imperial	*Metric*	*American*
Minced shoulder lamb	*1 lb*	*400 g*	*2 cups*
Packet Mince Savour, made up	*1*	*1*	*1*
Dried mint	*3/4 tsp*	*3/4 tsp*	*3/4 tsp*
Onion, large	*1*	*1*	*1*
Salt and pepper			

Sauce

Canned tomatoes	*14 oz*	*350 g*	*1 3/4 cup*
Onion	*1*	*1*	*1*
Mushroom, sliced	*2 oz*	*50 g*	*5/8 cup*
Green pepper (optional)	*1/2*	*1/2*	*1/2*
Stock	*1/4 pint*	*125 ml*	*5/8 cup*
Flour	*1 oz*	*25 g*	*1/4 cup*

Mix together the lamb, Mince Savour, mint, grated onion and seasonings. Shape into twelve meat balls. Place them in a large ovenware dish. To make the sauce, slice the onion and mushrooms and pepper. Blend all the sauce ingredients together except for the flour and heat gently. Mix the flour with a little cold water and pour the sauce on to this. Mix well and return to the pan. Allow to simmer for 10 minutes. Pour the sauce over the meat balls and bake covered in the oven at 350°F/180°C/Gas Mark 4 for $1\frac{1}{2}$ hours.

Serve with spaghetti, macaroni or rice.

Cheesy Shepherd's Pie

	Imperial	*Metric*	*American*
Minced cooked lamb	*1½ lb*	*600 g*	*4½ cups*
Mixed herbs	*1 tsp*	*1 tsp*	*1 tsp*
Carrots, large	*2*	*2*	*2*
Onion; large	*1*	*1*	*1*
Oil	*1 tbsp*	*1 tbsp*	*1 tbsp*
Mushrooms	*1 oz*	*25 g*	*¼ cup*
Stock	*3 tbsp*	*3 tbsp*	*3 tbsp*
Salt and pepper			
Potatoes	*1½ lb*	*600 g*	*1½ lb*
Cheddar cheese, grated	*1 oz*	*25 g*	*⅜ cup*

Mix together meat and seasoning. Fry finely chopped onion and carrot until soft but not brown. Mix all ingredients together except for potato and cheese. Put into an ovenware 3 pint/1½ litre/7-8 cup pie dish. Mash the potato and pipe it on top of the meat and cook at 350°F/180°C/Gas Mark 4 for 45 minutes. Ten minutes before completion of cooking time, top with grated cheese and return to the oven.

Serve with peas or beans, and carrots or parsnips.
Drink red wine or beer.
Follow with fruit baked in the same oven, or fresh fruit.

Chapter Five

FARAWAY PLACES

Minced beef lends itself to wonderfully exotic flavours, and all over the world there are delicious national dishes made with mince. Mince is good to use for stuffing Mediterranean peppers and aubergines, for livening up pasta, and for producing spicy curry and sweet-and-sour dishes. Tomatoes, onions, garlic and herbs enhance these rich dishes which taste just as good in colder northern climates.

Italian Stuffed Peppers

	Imperial	*Metric*	*American*
Green peppers	*4*	*4*	*4*
Onion, small	*1*	*1*	*1*
Raw minced beef	*4 oz*	*100 g*	*½ cup*
Butter	*1½ oz*	*40 g*	*⅛ cup+ 1 tbsp*
Tomatoes	*4*	*4*	*4*
Cooked rice	*4 oz*	*100 g*	*1½ cups*
Salt and pepper			
Cheese, grated	*4 tbsp*	*4 tbsp*	*4 tbsp*
Breadcrumbs	*2 oz*	*50 g*	*½ cup*
Stock	*¼ pint*	*125 ml*	*⅝ cup*

Cut peppers in half lengthwise and remove seeds. Put peppers in an ovenware dish. Fry chopped onion and minced beef until brown in 1 oz/25 g butter. Add rice, tomatoes, seasoning and half the cheese. Mix the remaining cheese with breadcrumbs. Put the meat stuffing into each pepper case and cover with breadcrumb mixture. Pour stock into dish. Top each pepper with butter and bake in centre of oven at 375°F/190°C/Gas Mark 5 for 20 minutes or until peppers are cooked.

Spanish Style Peppers

	Imperial	*Metric*	*American*
Raw minced beef	*12 oz*	*300 g*	*1½ cups*
Carrot, diced	*1*	*1*	*1*
Onion, medium	*1*	*1*	*1*
Green peppers	*4*	*4*	*4*
Tomato purée	*1 tbsp*	*1 tbsp*	*1 tbsp*
Arrowroot			
Can of tomatoes, large	*1*	*1*	*1*
Salt and pepper			
Cheese, grated	*2 oz*	*50 g*	*¾ cup*

Pre-heat the oven to 375°F/190°C/Gas Mark 5. Simmer the mince in saucepan and add finely chopped onion and carrot. Remove stalk and a slice from the base of each pepper so it will stand upright and de-seed. Put peppers in a pan. Cover with cold water. Bring to the boil and simmer for 15 minutes. Drain well. Stand the peppers in a dish and fill with the mince mixture. Blend a little of the tomato juice from the tin with a little arrowroot. Stir in the rest of the tomatoes. Boil, stirring continuously. Season. Spoon mixture around the base of the peppers. Cover dish with a lid or foil and bake in the centre of the preheated oven for 25 minutes, or until cooked. About 5 minutes before serving, cover each pepper with grated cheese. Pop back into oven until golden brown.

Serve on a bed of boiled rice.

Sweet and Sour Meat Balls

	Imperial	*Metric*	*American*
Minced beef	*1 lb*	*450 g*	*2 cups*
Salt	*1 tsp*	*1 tsp*	*1 tsp*
Cornflour	*1 tbsp*	*1 tbsp*	*1 tbsp*
Oil to fry			

Sauce

Green pepper	*1*	*1*	*1*
Cornflour	*1 tbsp*	*1 tbsp*	*1 tbsp*
Brown sugar	*1 tbsp*	*1 tbsp*	*1 tbsp*
Soy sauce	*2 tsp*	*2 tsp*	*2 tsp*
Chicken stock	*½ pint*	*250 ml*	*1¼ cups*
Vinegar	*¼ pint*	*125 ml*	*⅝ cup*
Sweet mustard pickle, pieces	*8*	*8*	*8*
Pineapple, slices	*3*	*3*	*3*

Season minced beef with salt and form into balls the size of walnuts. Roll in cornflour, and toss in hot oil for about 5 minutes. Cut the pepper into eight large pieces. Put stock and pepper into pan and simmer for 5 minutes or until pepper is tender. Mix cornflour, brown sugar, soy sauce together smoothly, and stir into stock. Cook for 3 minutes. Cut pickle and pineapple into small pieces and add to the sauce. Pour over the meat balls. Serve hot with more pickle.

Serve with boiled rice or with noodles.
Drink white wine or lager, or China tea without milk.
Follow with fresh fruit, or preserved ginger or lychees.

French Tomato Beef Pie

	Imperial	*Metric*	*American*
Onions	*8 oz*	*200 g*	*½ lb*
Fat	*1 oz*	*25 g*	*⅛ cup*
Flour	*1 oz*	*25 g*	*¼ cup*
Raw minced beef	*1 lb*	*450 g*	*2 cups*
Water	*½ pint*	*250 ml*	*1¼ cups*
Bayleaf	*1*	*1*	*1*
Thyme	*1 tsp*	*1 tsp*	*1 tsp*
Celery, small stick, chopped	*1*	*1*	*1*
Tomatoes	*8 oz*	*200 g*	*½ lb*
Potatoes, mashed	*8 oz*	*200 g*	*½ lb*
Egg	*1*	*1*	*1*
Flaked roasted almonds	*2 oz*	*50 g*	*¼ cup*

Fry sliced onions in fat until soft and brown. Sprinkle with flour and cook for 3 minutes. Add meat and blend well with onions. Season to taste and cover with hot water. Add bayleaf, thyme and celery and simmer for 30 minutes. Skin, seed and chop tomatoes and cook in a saucepan with a little fat until of a thick purée consistency. Place meat mixture in a pie dish. Beat potato while hot with an egg, and use to pipe circles over meat leaving centre free. Place tomato purée in centre. Sprinkle with almonds and brown at 400°F/200°C/Gas Mark 6 for 10 minutes.

Serve with peas or beans, or with a green side salad.
Drink red wine or lager.
Follow with baked apples filled with fruit mincemeat.

Stuffed Vine Leaves

	Imperial	*Metric*	*American*
Packet of vine leaves	*1*	*1*	*1*
Oil	*3 tbsp*	*3 tbsp*	*3 tbsp*
Raw minced beef	*1 lb*	*450 g*	*2 cups*
Onion	*1*	*1*	*1*
Cooked rice	*1 oz*	*25 g*	*⅓ cup+ 2 tbsp*
Parsley, chopped			
Tomato purée	*1 tsp*	*1 tsp*	*1 tsp*
Salt and pepper			
Juice of lemon	*1*	*1*	*1*

Dip the vine leaves in boiling water for 2 minutes and leave in a colander while you prepare the stuffing. Put 2 tablespoons oil in a frying pan with the meat, sliced onion, rice, parsley, tomato purée and seasoning. Mix well and fry. Stuff the vine leaves with this mixture and secure with fine string or skewers. Put in a saucepan with a little water and the remaining oil. Cook over a low heat until remaining sauce has reduced, and until leaves are tender.

Aubergines, peppers and tomatoes may also be filled with this stuffing.

Serve with rice or noodles, and follow with green salad.
Drink dry white wine or cider.
Follow with treacle tart or baklava (honey-soaked pastry squares).

Quick Moussaka

	Imperial	*Metric*	*American*
Cooked potatoes, sliced	*12 oz*	*300 g*	*¾ lb*
Cooked minced beef	*12 oz*	*300 g*	*2¼ cups*
Tomatoes, skinned, sliced	*2*	*2*	*2*
A little parsley, chopped			
Butter or margarine	*1 oz*	*25 g*	*⅛ cup*
Flour	*1 oz*	*25 g*	*¼ cup*
Milk	*½ pint*	*250 ml*	*1¼ cups*
Salt and pepper			
Cheese, grated	*3 oz*	*75 g*	*1⅛ cups*

Arrange layers of potatoes in a greased pie dish. Put the meat, sliced tomatoes and parsley on top of the potatoes. Cover with another layer of potatoes. Melt the butter or margarine, stir in the flour and cook for several minutes. Gradually add milk and boil until thick and smooth. Stir in most of the cheese and seasoning and pour over the mixture. Sprinkle with grated cheese. Cook for 40 minutes at 400°F/200°C/Gas Mark 6, until golden brown on top. Garnish with parsley and more sliced tomatoes.

Serve with spinach or broccoli, or with a green salad.
Drink red wine or beer.
Follow with apples or plums cooked in the oven with sugar.

Moussaka

	Imperial	*Metric*	*American*
Aubergines	*6*	*6*	*6*
Cooked minced beef	*1 lb*	*400 g*	*3 cups*
Tomato puree	*1 tbsp*	*1 tbsp*	*1 tbsp*
Onions	*8 oz*	*200 g*	*½ lb*
Oil	*3 fl. oz*	*75 ml*	*⅜ cup*
Breadcrumbs	*1 oz*	*25 g*	*¼ cup*
Parsley, chopped	*1 tbsp*	*1 tbsp*	*1 tbsp*
Eggs	*2*	*2*	*2*

Keep 2 aubergines in reserve and slice them without peeling. Split the remaining 4 lengthways leaving the skin on. Fry in deep fat for 5 minutes, remove, drain and scoop out pulp. Line the bottom and sides of a shallow dish with the aubergine skins placing the coloured side against the mould. Mix some chopped aubergine and meat and add the chopped onions. Add parsley, tomato purée and breadcrumbs. Season with salt and pepper. Blend the mixture with the two beaten eggs. Place layer of mixture, then layer of aubergines kept in reserve. Build up layers in the dish until all the mixture and aubergines have been used. Cover with cooking foil and cook for 1 hour in a tin of water at 350°F/180°C/Gas Mark 4. When cooked, invert the dish and turn out. Serve with tossed salad and tomato sauce if required.

A cheese sauce may be served instead.

Creole Macaroni

	Imperial	Metric	American
Onions	2	2	2
Green or red pepper	1	1	1
Butter	2 oz	50 g	1/4 cup
Stock	1/4 pint	125 ml	5/8 cup
Cooked minced beef	8 oz	200 g	1 1/2 cups
Tomatoes	4	4	4
Quick-cooking macaroni	6 oz	150 g	3/4 cup
Salt and pepper			

Fry sliced onions and pepper in the butter. Add the stock, minced beef and tomatoes and heat thoroughly. Cook the macaroni for 7 minutes in boiling water. Strain and mix with the meat mixture. Serve at once.

Russian Poached Pasties

	Imperial	Metric	American
Flour	8 oz	200 g	2 cups
Salt	1/2 tsp	1/2 tsp	1/2 tsp
Egg yolks	2	2	2
Melted butter	1 tbsp	1 tbsp	1 tbsp
Cold water			
Cooked mince	6 oz	150 g	1 1/8 cups
Sage	1 tsp	1 tsp	1 tsp
Onion, small	1	1	1
Pinch of curry powder			

Sift flour with salt, egg yolks, melted butter and enough water to mix to a stiff paste. Roll out thinly. Cut into 3 in./7 cm circles. Season the mince with sage, chopped onion and curry powder. Spread one round with minced beef, top with another round and seal edges by pressing firmly together after brushing with cold water. Poach in boiling water for about 15 minutes. Serve hot, with melted butter.

Hungarian Style Casserole

	Imperial	*Metric*	*American*
Marjoram	*½ tsp*	*½ tsp*	*½ tsp*
Parsley, chopped	*½ tsp*	*½ tsp*	*½ tsp*
Raw minced beef	*1½ lb*	*675 g*	*3 cups*
Salt and pepper			
Onion, small	*1*	*1*	*1*
Flour	*1½ oz*	*40 g*	*¼ cup+ 2 tbsp*
Paprika	*1 tbsp*	*1 tbsp*	*1 tbsp*
Tomato purée	*1 tbsp*	*1 tbsp*	*1 tbsp*
Beef stock cube	*1*	*1*	*1*
Boiling water	*¾ pint*	*375 ml*	*1⅞ cups*
Potatoes, medium	*2*	*2*	*2*
Cooked ham	*2 oz*	*50 g*	*⅜ cup*
Soured cream	*3 fl. oz*	*75 ml*	*⅜ cup*

Pre-heat the oven to 325°F/170°C/Gas Mark 3. Mix marjoram and chopped parsley with the meat and fry. Drain off the fat. Season and stir in the chopped onion, flour and paprika. Add the purée and stock cube dissolved in water. Bring to the boil. Put in casserole. Cover and cook in the centre of the oven for 2 hours. Add peeled and diced potatoes and strips of ham 25 minutes before the end of cooking. Just before serving, add the cream.

Serve with plainly-boiled potatoes.
Drink beer or cider.
Follow with a bowl of sliced oranges sprinkled with sugar.

Polish Style Beef

	Imperial	Metric	American
Onion	*1*	*1*	*1*
Cooking fat or oil	*2 oz*	*50 g*	*1/4 cup*
Minced beef	*1 lb*	*450 g*	*2 cups*
Tomato purée	*1 tbsp*	*1 tbsp*	*1 tbsp*
Salt and pepper			
Breadcrumbs	*10 oz*	*250 g*	*2 1/2 cups*
Butter	*3 oz*	*75 g*	*3/8 cup*
Hard-boiled eggs	*2*	*2*	*2*
Chopped parsley			
Cheese, grated	*2 oz*	*50 g*	*3/4 cup*

Fry the chopped onion in the fat or oil until clear, remove from the pan and cook the meat for 20 minutes. Add tomato purée, onion, salt and pepper. Fry the breadcrumbs in butter until golden brown. Finely chop the eggs, and add to the breadcrumbs, parsley and cheese. Place mince in a serving dish and cover with the breadcrumb mixture. Place under a grill or in a moderate oven for 10–15 minutes until crisp.

Serve with chips and peas or beans, and a bowl of beetroot in vinegar.
Drink beer or cider.
Follow with pineapple or banana or apple fritters and cinnamon sugar.

Minced Beef American-Style

	Imperial	*Metric*	*American*
Onion, large	*1*	*1*	*1*
Salt belly of pork (soaked in cold water for 4 hours)	*8 oz*	*200 g*	*½ lb*
Raw minced beef	*1 lb*	*400 g*	*2 cups*
Salt and pepper			
Soft brown sugar	*1 tbsp*	*1 tbsp*	*1 tbsp*
Black treacle or molasses	*1 tsp*	*1 tsp*	*1 tsp*
Dry mustard	*1 tbsp*	*1 tbsp*	*1 tbsp*
Vinegar	*1 tbsp*	*1 tbsp*	*1 tbsp*
Beef stock cube	*1*	*1*	*1*
Boiling water	*¾ pint*	*375 ml*	*1⅞ cups*
Pinch of garlic salt			
Pinch of turmeric			
Pinch of cinnamon			
Flour	*1 oz*	*25 g*	*¼ cup*
Haricot beans, fresh or canned	*1 lb*	*400 g*	*1 lb*

Chop the onion. Cut up drained pork and put in a pan with the onion. Add beef, salt and pepper, sugar, treacle, mustard vinegar stock, garlic salt, turmeric and cinnamon. Put lid on the pan and simmer for 1¾ hours or until pork is tender, stirring occasionally. When cooked, allow to become quite cold. Skim fat off the surface. Reheat and thicken with flour. Drain canned beans and stir into the stew. Reheat for 2 minutes. If fresh haricot beans are used, they must be soaked and should be added 45 minutes before the end of cooking.

Serve very hot with jacket potatoes.

Brazilian Minced Beef

	Imperial	Metric	American
Oil	*2 tbsp*	*2 tbsp*	*2 tbsp*
Onion, medium	*1*	*1*	*1*
Raw minced beef	*1 lb*	*400 g*	*2 cups*
Mixed herbs	*2 tsp*	*2 tsp*	*2 tsp*
Egg	*1*	*1*	*1*
Cornflour	*1 oz*	*25 g*	*¼ cup*
Packet tomato soup	*1*	*1*	*1*
Water	*1¼ pints*	*625 ml*	*3⅛ cups*
Sherry	*1 tbsp*	*1 tbsp*	*1 tbsp*
Red wine	*1 tbsp*	*1 tbsp*	*1 tbsp*
Broad or lima beans, fresh or frozen	*1 lb*	*400 g*	*1 lb*
Mashed potatoes	*1 lb*	*400 g*	*4 cups*

Heat the oil, and cook onions until soft. Remove from the pan. Mix with beef, herbs and egg. Form the mixture into balls and coat with the cornflour. Return the meatballs to the pan with remaining oil and brown. Remove from the pan. Add contents of packet soup, water, sherry and wine and bring to boil. Replace the meatballs, cover and simmer gently for 25 minutes. Line an ovenware dish with mashed potatoes and pipe in a decorative-style. Brown under the grill. Cook and strain the broad beans. Pile meatballs into centre of the potato case with a little of the sauce. Surround with broad beans and serve the remaining sauce separately.

Sprinkle the top with a little chopped parsley.

Minced Beef Stroganoff

	Imperial	*Metric*	*American*
Raw minced beef	*1½ lb*	*675 g*	*3 cups*
Beef stock cube	*1*	*1*	*1*
Boiling water	*½ pint*	*250 ml*	*1¼ cups*
Canned tomato juice	*3 fl. oz*	*75 ml*	*⅜ cup*
Onion, small	*1*	*1*	*1*
Mushrooms	*3 oz*	*75 g*	*1 cup*
Basil	*1 tsp*	*1 tsp*	*1 tsp*
Flour	*1½ oz*	*40 g*	*¼ cup+ 2 tbsp*
Salt and pepper			
Soured cream	*5 fl. oz*	*125 ml*	*⅝ cup*

Put the meat into a pan and fry gently, then drain off excess fat. Add stock, tomato juice, chopped onion, mushrooms and basil. Simmer with the lid on the pan for 1 hour or until mince is well cooked. Stir occasionally. Put flour in a cup and stir in 4 tablespoons cold water. Pour into the pan. Bring to the boil, stirring until thickened. Season to taste. Serve very hot with cream on top.

Serve with boiled rice, and a green salad to follow.
Drink red wine or beer.
Follow with fruit water ice or fresh fruit.

Creole Canneloni

	Imperial	Metric	American
Onion, medium	1	1	1
Minced beef	12 oz	300 g	1½ cups
Garlic clove	½–1	½–1	½–1
Canned tomatoes	7 oz	175 g	⅞ cup
Tomato purée	1 tbsp	1 tbsp	1 tbsp
Chopped chives	2 tbsp	2 tbsp	2 tbsp
Stock	¼ pint	125 ml	⅝ cup
Salt and pepper			
Square canneloni	8	8	8
Butter	1 oz	25 g	⅛ cup
Flour	1 oz	25 g	¼ cup
Milk	½ pint	250 ml	1¼ cups
Cheese, grated	3 oz	75 g	1⅛ cups

Fry the chopped onion until brown, reduce the heat, add the meat and cook for 5 minutes. Add tomatoes, crushed garlic, tomato purée and chives, salt and pepper. Cover pan and cook slowly for 30–40 minutes. Cook canneloni as directed on the packet and leave in cold water to cool. Divide mixture equally on to the 8 slices of canneloni. Roll up and place in an ovenware dish. Put butter in a saucepan and melt on low heat. Stir in the flour and milk and cook until smooth and thick. Stir in two-thirds of the cheese and pour the sauce over the canneloni. Sprinkle on the remaining cheese. Bake at 400°F/200°C/Gas Mark 6 for 30 minutes.

Serve with a green salad to follow.

Russian-Style Minced Beef

	Imperial	*Metric*	*American*
Cooking oil	*1 tbsp*	*1 tbsp*	*1 tbsp*
Raw minced beef	*8 oz*	*200 g*	*1 cup*
Onion, large	*1*	*1*	*1*
Potatoes, boiled	*8 oz*	*200 g*	*½ lb*
Kipper, boned and cooked	*3 oz*	*75 g*	*⅜ cup*
Salt and pepper			
Egg	*1*	*1*	*1*
Milk	*¼ pint*	*125 ml*	*⅝ cup*
Brown breadcrumbs	*4 oz*	*100 g*	*1 cup*
Dill	*½ tsp*	*½ tsp*	*½ tsp*
Rosemary	*½ tsp*	*½ tsp*	*½ tsp*

Pre-heat oven to 350°F/180°C/Gas Mark 4. Heat oil and cook onions until soft but not brown. Remove onion from frying pan and cook minced beef for 20 minutes. Boil the potatoes, drain and mash. Add kipper, dill, rosemary to minced beef, season to taste, mix well. Add beaten egg to mixture and hot milk to make mixture pliable and light. Grease a pie dish, fill with mixture, sprinkle top with brown breadcrumbs and bake for 20 minutes.

Serve with broccoli or cauliflower, and dill cucumbers.
Drink lager or cider.
Follow with fresh fruit and cheese.

Spaghetti Bolognese

	Imperial	*Metric*	*American*
Spaghetti	*8 oz*	*200 g*	*½ lb*
Parmesan cheese			
Bacon rashers	*4*	*4*	*4*
Butter	*½ oz*	*12 g*	*1 tbsp*
Onion, small	*1*	*1*	*1*
Celery stick	*1*	*1*	*1*
Carrot, medium	*1*	*1*	*1*
Minced beef	*8 oz*	*200 g*	*1 cup*
Tomato purée	*1 tbsp*	*1 tsp*	*1 tbsp*
Dry white wine	*¼ pint*	*125 ml*	*⅝ cup*
Beef stock	*½ pint*	*250 ml*	*1¼ cups*
Salt and pepper			

Fry chopped bacon lightly in butter for 3 minutes. Add chopped onion, celery and carrot and fry for 5 minutes until brown. Add beef and brown. Add tomato purée and wine and allow to boil for a few minutes. Add stock and seasoning. Simmer for 40 minutes until meat is tender and liquid well reduced. Add more seasoning if required. Serve with spaghetti. Sprinkle cheese over the sauce.

Serve with a green side salad.
Drink red wine or lager.
Follow with sliced fresh pineapple or oranges.

Spaghetti with Meat Balls

	Imperial	Metric	American
Raw minced beef	*1 lb*	*450 g*	*2 cups*
Garlic clove	*½–1*	*½–1*	*½–1*
Thick slice of bread, soaked in milk	*1*	*1*	*1*
Mixed herbs	*½ tsp*	*½ tsp*	*½ tsp*
Pinch of nutmeg			
Salt and pepper			
Egg	*1*	*1*	*1*
Butter for frying			

Sauce

Celery sticks	*2*	*2*	*2*
Onion	*8 oz*	*200 g*	*½ lb*
Mushrooms, chopped	*2 oz*	*50 g*	*⅝ cup*
Tomatoes, medium can	*1*	*1*	*1*
Tomato purée	*2 tbsp*	*2 tbsp*	*2 tbsp*
Sugar	*1 tsp*	*1 tsp*	*1 tsp*
Salt and pepper			
Basil	*½ tsp*	*½ tsp*	*½ tsp*

Meatballs: Chop the celery finely and crush the garlic. Mix all the ingredients (except the celery) and bind them with egg. Turn mixture on to floured surface. Divide into 15 pieces and form into balls. Fry in butter for about 5 minutes until golden brown and remove from pan.

The sauce: Fry chopped onion, celery and mushrooms in same fat as meatballs for 5 minutes or until soft. Stir in remaining ingredients for the sauce and add meat balls. Cover and simmer for 30 minutes or until sauce is cooked and meatballs are tender.

Serve with spaghetti cooked in the normal way.

Dutch Beef Pancakes

	Imperial	*Metric*	*American*
Flour	*8 oz*	*200 g*	*2 cups*
Salt	*1 tsp*	*1 tsp*	*1 tsp*
Fresh yeast			
(or dried equivalent)	*½ oz*	*12 g*	*2 tbsp*
Sugar	*1 tsp*	*1 tsp*	*1 tsp*
Milk	*1 pint*	*500 ml*	*2½ cups*
Beaten egg	*1*	*1*	*1*
Cooked minced beef	*4 oz*	*100 g*	*¾ cup*
Chopped parsley			

Sift the flour and salt together. Cream yeast with sugar. Warm milk slightly. Make a hole in middle of flour and add yeast mixture mixed with half the milk and egg. Beat well and leave to rise for 20 minutes. Work in rest of milk and beat well. Cover mixture with cloth and leave for 1 hour. Heat minced beef. Make pancakes, put meat mixture on one half, fold and place in warm dish. Serve hot, garnished with chopped parsley.

Serve with peas or beans, and pickles.
Drink beer or cider.
Follow with baked or refrigerated cheesecake.

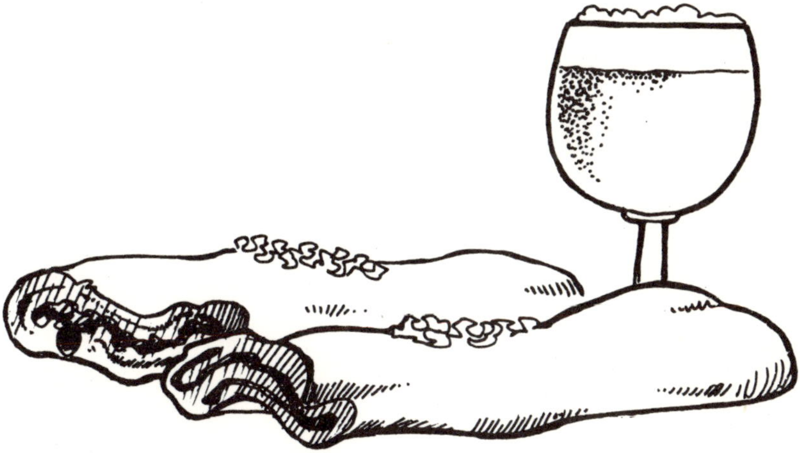

Smyrna Sausage

	Imperial	Metric	American
White bread, slices	*2*	*2*	*2*
Milk			
Raw minced beef	*1 lb*	*450 g*	*2 cups*
Onions	*2*	*2*	*2*
Chopped parsley			
A little mint and basil			
Cumin powder	*¼ tsp*	*¼ tsp*	*¼ tsp*
Egg, beaten	*1*	*1*	*1*
Flour	*2 oz*	*50 g*	*½ cup*
Tomato purée	*10 tbsp*	*10 tbsp*	*10 tbsp*
Sugar	*½ oz*	*12 g*	*1 tbsp*
White wine	*6 fl. oz*	*150 ml*	*¾ cup*
Water	*¼ pint*	*125 ml*	*⅝ cup*
Salt and pepper			

Cut off crusts and then soak bread in milk. Squeeze almost dry. Place meat in a basin and mix with half chopped onion and the soaked bread, chopped herbs and cumin powder. Bind the mixture with the egg and knead well. Roll into small sausage shapes about 2 in./5 cm. long and fry lightly in oil or butter until meat is pale golden brown. Place carefully in a saucepan. Prepare tomato sauce by frying remaining diced onion until soft and transparent, adding flour and tomato purée, sugar, wine, water, salt and pepper. Simmer for a few minutes. Pour over sausage and simmer for 45 minutes until meat is cooked.

Serve with boiled rice.

Lasagne

	Imperial	*Metric*	*American*
Raw minced beef	*1 lb*	*450 g*	*2 cups*
Marjoram or sage	*1 tsp*	*1 tsp*	*1 tsp*
Onion, small	*1*	*1*	*1*
Tomato puree	*1 tbsp*	*1 tbsp*	*1 tbsp*
Beef stock cube	*1*	*1*	*1*
Boiling water	*½ pint*	*250 ml*	*1¼ cups*
Salt and pepper			
Flour	*2 oz*	*50 g*	*½ cup*
Wide ribbon noodles	*10 oz*	*250 g*	*3 cups*
Butter	*1 oz*	*25 g*	*⅛ cup*
Milk, quantities less 4 tablespoons	*½ pint*	*250 ml*	*1⅛ cups*
Single cream	*4 tbsp*	*4 tbsp*	*4 tbsp*
Small egg yolk	*1*	*1*	*1*
Cheddar cheese, grated	*3 oz*	*75 g*	*1⅛ cup*

To prepare meat sauce: Put meat in a pan and fry gently. Drain off as much of the fat as you can. Stir in the herbs and chopped onion. Fry for 2 minutes. Add purée and stock. Put lid on pan and simmer for 50 minutes, stirring occasionally. Season to taste. Blend 1 oz/25 g/ ¼ cup flour with 4 tablespoons cold water. Add to pan and boil, stirring, until thickened. Meanwhile, cook noodles in boiling salted water for 15 minutes.

Heat oven to 325°F/170°C/Gas Mark 3.

White sauce: melt butter in a pan, add the rest of the flour. Cook gently for 1 minute. Gradually stir in the milk until smooth. Boil, stirring until thick. Remove from heat. Stir in cream, egg yolk and cheese. Put meat and noodles in ovenproof dish in layers. Pour sauce over top to cover and bake, uncovered, in the centre of the oven for 45 minutes, or until browned. Serve hot with salad.

Greek Spicy Meat Balls

	Imperial	*Metric*	*American*
Raw minced beef	*1 lb*	*450 g*	*2 cups*
Fresh white breadcrumbs	*2 oz*	*50 g*	*1⅓ cups*
Lemon, small	*1*	*1*	*1*
Garlic clove	*½–1*	*½–1*	*½–1*
Black pepper			
Marjoram	*1 tsp*	*1 tsp*	*1 tsp*
Parsley, chopped	*1 tsp*	*1 tsp*	*1 tsp*
Good pinch of cinnamon			
Onion, small	*1*	*1*	*1*
Egg	*1*	*1*	*1*
Oil for frying			

Put minced beef in a bowl with the breadcrumbs. Cut half the lemon into slices. Squeeze the juice from the other half and add to the meat with crushed garlic, pepper, marjoram, parsley and cinnamon. Chop the onion and stir in. Mix all the ingredients together and bind with the egg. Shape into 12 balls. Leave in a cold place for 20 minutes. Heat the oil in a pan. Fry the balls for 20 minutes, turning them as they cook. Drain on paper, and serve with lemon slices.

Serve with boiled rice, and a green salad to follow.
Drink dry white wine.
Follow with baklava (honey-soaked pastry squares) or walnut cake.

Dutch Yeast Pancakes

	Imperial	Metric	American
Flour	5½ oz	138 g	1⅓ cups
Fresh yeast or dried equivalent	¼ oz	6 g	1 tbsp
Milk	½ pint	250 ml	1¼ cups
Eggs, large	1	1	1
Raw minced beef	1 lb	450 g	2 cups
Salt and pepper			
Pinch of basil			
Can of tomatoes, small	1	1	1
Tomato purée	2 tbsp	2 tbsp	2 tbsp
Streaky bacon rashers	2	2	2
Beef stock cube	1	1	1
Boiling water	¼ pint	125 ml	⅝ cup
Dried mixed herbs	1 tsp	1 tsp	1 tsp
Oil or lard to fry pancakes			

Sift 4 oz/ 100 g/1 cup flour into a bowl. Mix yeast with a little of the milk and add to flour with half the rest of the milk and the egg. Beat well. Cover and leave in a warm place for 20 minutes. Add the rest of the milk with a wooden spoon and beat well. Cover and leave for 1 hour.

To make the meat sauce, fry the meat, then drain off fat. Add salt and pepper, basil, tomatoes, tomato purée, chopped bacon, stock cube and water and herbs. Put a lid on the pan and simmer for 45 minutes until the meat is well cooked, stirring occasionally. When prepared, thicken with rest of the flour in the usual way. Take a little lard or oil and heat in a large frying pan and pour off excess. Make 4 pancakes cooking for about 2 minutes on each side, having the batter thicker than normal. When cooked, serve flat topped with meat sauce.

Greek Beef and Potato Cake

	Imperial	Metric	American
Raw minced beef	*12 oz*	*300 g*	*1½ cups*
Onion, sliced	*8 oz*	*200 g*	*½ lb*
Parsley, chopped	*1 tsp*	*1 tsp*	*1 tsp*
Water	*¼ pint*	*125 ml*	*⅝ cup*
Margarine	*2 oz*	*50 g*	*¼ cup*
Tomatoes	*8 oz*	*200 g*	*½ lb*
Potatoes	*2 lb*	*1 kg*	*2 lb*
Salt and pepper			
Butter	*½ oz*	*12 g*	*1 tbsp*
Flour	*½ oz*	*12 g*	*2 tbsp*
Milk	*¼ pint*	*125 ml*	*⅝ cup*
Egg	*1*	*1*	*1*
Cheese, grated	*1 oz*	*25 g*	*⅜ cup*

Put meat, onions and parsley in a frying pan with water and simmer until all the water has been absorbed. Add margarine and cook gently, then add skinned and sliced tomatoes and season well. Cook slowly for 20 minutes. Grease a cake tin or oblong casserole dish. Place a layer of thinly sliced potatoes on the bottom, then a layer of meat mixture. Repeat layers finishing with a potato layer. Make a white sauce with the butter, flour and milk. Remove from the heat and beat in the egg and cheese. Pour over the potato and bake at 350°F/180°C/Gas Mark 4 for 1 hour.

Serve with spinach or broccoli, or a green salad.
Drink red wine or beer.
Follow with a fresh fruit salad sweetened with honey.

Minced Beef Kebabs

	Imperial	*Metric*	*American*
Raw minced beef	*1 lb*	*450 g*	*2 cups*
White breadcrumbs	*3 oz*	*75 g*	*2 cups*
Dried marjoram	*2 tsp*	*2 tsp*	*2 tsp*
Salt	*1 tsp*	*1 tsp*	*1 tsp*
Black pepper			
Tomato purée	*1 tbsp*	*1 tbsp*	*1 tbsp*
Egg	*1*	*1*	*1*
Button mushrooms	*4 oz*	*100 g*	*1¼ cups*
Green pepper	*1*	*1*	*1*
Button onions	*6 oz*	*150 g*	*⅞ cup*
Cooking oil			
Tomatoes	*8 oz*	*200 g*	*½ lb*
Bacon rashers	*3*	*3*	*3*

Mix beef with the breadcrumbs, marjoram, salt and pepper and tomato purée. Bind with the beaten egg. Roll the mixture into 20 balls. Thread the meatballs and mushrooms, sliced pepper and onions on to 8 long skewers. Brush with oil and place under a hot grill until golden. While cooking, turn frequently and brush with more oil. Halfway through, put tomatoes on to the end of the skewers – if really small tomatoes are available use these whole, otherwise use quartered tomatoes. When the kebabs are almost cooked, prepare bacon into small rolls and slot on to skewers and cook until bacon is crispy.

Serve with tomato sauce and a green salad.

Indian Pie

	Imperial	Metric	American
Cooking fat	1 oz	25 g	1/8 cup
Onions, chopped	8 oz	200 g	1/2 lb
Curry powder	1 oz	200 g	2 tbsp
Vinegar	1 tbsp	1 tbsp	1 tbsp
Tomato purée	1 oz	25 g	2 1/2 tbsp
Stock or water	2 tbsp	2 tbsp	2 tbsp
Raw minced beef	12 oz	300 g	1 1/2 cups
Mashed potatoes	1 1/2 lb	600 g	6 cups
Parsley			
Tomato	1	1	1

Heat the fat and fry the onions until golden. Add the curry powder and vinegar and continue frying for 5 minutes. Add the tomato purée, stock or water and meat and continue cooking for 10 minutes. Turn into a casserole brushed with fat and cover with mashed potatoes. Bake at 400°F/200°C/Gas Mark 6 for 30 minutes. Garnish with parsley and tomato slices.

Turkish Pilau

	Imperial	Metric	American
Cooked minced beef	1 lb	450 g	3 cups
Onion, small	1	1	1
Tomato	1	1	1
Cooked celery sticks	2	2	2
Boiled rice	12 oz	300 g	6 3/4 cups
Beef stock	3/4 pint	375 ml	1 7/8 cups
Breadcrumbs	6 oz	150 g	1 1/2 cups
Melted butter	2 oz	50 g	1/4 cup
Salt and pepper			

Mix rice, minced onion, sliced tomato and chopped celery, and stock. Season and arrange in alternate layers with meat in a greased casserole. Cover with breadcrumbs which have been mixed with the melted butter. Bake at 350°F/180°C/Gas Mark 4 for 30 minutes.

Spanish Beef and Rice Casserole

	Imperial	*Metric*	*American*
Bacon rashers	*3*	*3*	*3*
Onion, medium	*1*	*1*	*1*
Raw minced beef	*1 lb*	*450 g*	*2 cups*
Salt and pepper			
Pinch of paprika			
Tomatoes, skinned, sliced	*1 lb*	*450 g*	*1 lb*
Rice	*4 oz*	*100 g*	*5/8 cup*
Tomato purée	*1 tsp*	*1 tsp*	*1 tsp*

Chop the bacon and fry gently, then remove from the pan. Slice the onion and brown in the bacon fat, then add beef, salt and pepper and paprika. Stir until the meat browns. Add tomatoes and tomato purée, bacon and rice. Put in a greased casserole, cover and cook at 350°F/180°C/Gas Mark 4 for 1 hour. Add a little water if it becomes too dry when cooking.

Minced Beef Chow Mein

	Imperial	*Metric*	*American*
Raw minced beef	*1 lb*	*450 g*	*2 cups*
Onions	*2*	*2*	*2*
Butter	*4 oz*	*100 g*	*1/2 cup*
Cabbage	*1/2*	*1/2*	*1/2*
Chicken noodle soup, packets	*2*	*2*	*2*
Water	*1 pint*	*500 ml*	*2 1/2 cups*
Curry powder	*1/2 oz*	*12 g*	*2 tbsp*
Sugar	*1 oz*	*12 g*	*1/8 cup*
Sultanas	*1 oz*	*25 g*	*1/4 cup*
Green beans, sliced	*8 oz*	*200 g*	*1/2 lb*
Soya sauce	*2 tsp*	*2 tsp*	*2 tsp*
Rice	*1 oz*	*25 g*	*1/8 cup*

Brown the mince and sliced onions together in butter. Add the rest of the ingredients and simmer for 25 minutes in a large saucepan, stirring occasionally.

Caribbean Beef Balls

	Imperial	Metric	American
Raw minced beef	1 lb	450 g	2 cups
Onions	2	2	2
Tomatoes	2	2	2
Salt and pepper			
Egg	1	1	1
Deep fat for frying			

Mix the beef, chopped onions, and tomatoes and season well with salt and pepper. Beat the egg well, add to the beef mixture and mix thoroughly. Form into 12 balls, and fry in deep fat until golden brown.

Carbonado

	Imperial	Metric	American
Butter	2 oz	50 g	1/4 cup
Onion, medium	4	4	4
Tomato	1	1	1
Raw minced beef	1 1/2 lb	675 g	3 cups
Salt and pepper			
Stock	1/4 pint	125 ml	5/8 cup
Pears	2	2	2
Peaches	2	2	2
Potatoes, medium	4	4	4
Seedless raisins	2 oz	50 g	1/2 cup

Heat butter in an ovenware casserole. Fry sliced onions until brown, add peeled and sliced tomato and fry for 2 minutes. Add beef, stir well and brown for 2 minutes. Add salt, pepper and stock. Cover and cook gently for 1 hour. Add peeled and sliced pears and peaches and diced potatoes and simmer for 20 minutes. Stir in raisins just before serving.

Indian Kafta

	Imperial	*Metric*	*American*
Onion, large	*2*	*2*	*2*
Raw minced beef	*1 lb*	*450 g*	*2 cups*
Curry powder	*1 oz*	*25 g*	*4 tbsp*
Garlic clove	*½–1*	*½–1*	*½–1*
Butter	*2 oz*	*50 g*	*¼ cup*
Salt			
Tomatoes	*1 lb*	*450 g*	*1 lb*
Beef stock	*½ pint*	*250 ml*	*1¼ cups*

Mince an onion and add to the meat together with half the curry powder. Knead and divide into small portions and roll into balls. Slice the second onion, chop the garlic and fry in the butter until just turning golden brown. Add the remaining curry powder, salt and quartered tomatoes, and stock and leave to cook for 2 minutes. Carefully add the meat balls, cover with a lid and cook gently for 30 minutes, taking care not to break the meatballs. Serve with rice.

Serve with chutney and with thinly-sliced cucumber in yogurt.
Drink lager or cider.
Follow with ice cream and small sweet biscuits.

Spanish Beef Loaf

	Imperial	*Metric*	*American*
Tomatoes	*2*	*2*	*2*
Raw minced beef	*1 lb*	*450 g*	*2 cups*
Garlic clove	*½–1*	*½–1*	*½–1*
Fresh white breadcrumbs	*2 oz*	*50 g*	*1⅓ cups*
Red peppers, chopped	*2 oz*	*50 g*	*½ cup*
Tomato purée	*2 oz*	*50 g*	*5 tbsp*
Basil	*1 tsp*	*1 tsp*	*1 tsp*
Tabasco sauce	*1 tsp*	*1 tsp*	*1 tsp*
Egg	*1*	*1*	*1*
Salt and pepper			

Slice the tomatoes and arrange them in the base of a greased loaf tin. Mix minced beef with the crushed garlic, breadcrumbs, tomato purée, basil and Tabasco, and bind with beaten egg. Season well with salt and pepper, press well into the tin, and smooth the top. Cover with foil and stand the loaf tin in a roasting tin with water reaching halfway up. Bake at 325°F/170°C/Gas Mark 3 for 1½ hours until firm. Turn out and serve hot.

Serve with green beans and mashed potatoes.
Drink beer or cider.
Follow with a bowl of mixed sliced oranges and pineapple.

Macaroni Layer

	Imperial	Metric	American
Onion, large	*1*	*1*	*1*
Cooking oil			
Raw minced beef	*1 lb*	*450 g*	*2 cups*
Salt and pepper			
Mushrooms, chopped	*4 oz*	*100 g*	*1¼ cups*
Mixed herbs	*½ tbsp*	*½ tbsp*	*½ tbsp*
Garlic clove	*½–1*	*½–1*	*½–1*
Macaroni	*1 lb*	*450 g*	*4 cups*
Tomatoes	*8 oz*	*200 g*	*½ lb*
Parmesan cheese			
Parsley, chopped	*½ tbsp*	*½ tbsp*	*½ tbsp*

Cook chopped onion in oil until clear and remove from pan. Brown beef, then simmer for 20 minutes. Remove from the heat and add the onion, salt and pepper, chopped mushrooms, herbs and crushed garlic. Stir the mixture until all ingredients are mixed. Cook the macaroni, drain and then layer macaroni and minced beef in an ovenware dish, finishing with a final layer of macaroni. Decorate with sliced tomatoes and sprinkle with Parmesan cheese. Bake at 425°F/220°C/Gas Mark 7 for 25 minutes. Decorate with chopped parsley.

Serve with a green salad to follow.

Curried Mince

	Imperial	*Metric*	*American*
Oil	*2 tbsp*	*2 tbsp*	*2 tbsp*
Cooking apple	*1*	*1*	*1*
Onions, medium	*2*	*2*	*2*
Curry powder	*2 tbsp*	*2 tbsp*	*2 tbsp*
Flour	*½ oz*	*12 g*	*2 tbsp*
Beef stock	*½ pint*	*250 ml*	*1¼ cups*
Chutney	*1 tbsp*	*1 tbsp*	*1 tbsp*
Sultanas	*2 oz*	*50 g*	*½ cup*
Raw minced beef	*1 lb*	*450 g*	*2 cups*

Lemon slices and parsley sprigs to garnish.

Heat oil and fry chopped apple and onions until brown. Remove from frying pan, drain well, and place in large saucepan. To the remaining fat add the curry powder and flour and cook for 2 minutes. Add the stock, bring to boil and cook for 2 minutes. Add the chutney and sultanas. Cook the mince in the remaining fat and add to the contents of the saucepan. Simmer the mince for 20 minutes. Serve with boiled rice and decorate with lemon slices and parsley sprigs.

Serve with a selection of chutneys, and a green salad to follow.
Drink lager or cider.
Follow with fresh fruit and cheese.

Chapter Six

SOMETHING SPECIAL

It is not always necessary to serve expensive and over-rich food to guests. Most friends are happier with familiar foods cooked in a rather special way, and minced beef can be just as acceptable for a company dinner as for a family meal. By using mince cleverly, it is possible to entertain more friends more often which is much more fun than having to save up for one lavish meal served rarely.

Scalloped Aubergines with Meat

	Imperial	*Metric*	*American*
Aubergine, large	*1*	*1*	*1*
Salt and pepper			
Raw minced beef	*1 lb*	*450 g*	*2 cups*
Onion	*1*	*1*	*1*
Parsley, chopped	*2 tbsp*	*2 tbsp*	*2 tbsp*
Mixed herbs	*½ tbsp*	*½ tbsp*	*½ tbsp*
Tomato purée	*2 oz*	*50 g*	*5 tbsp*
Water	*2 tbsp*	*2 tbsp*	*2 tbsp*

Cut the aubergine in thick slices and sprinkle with salt. Leave for 30 minutes and drain off liquid. Mix the beef with the chopped onion, parsley and herbs. Season well. Spread meat mixture on aubergine slices and arrange in a well greased ovenware dish. Mix tomato purée and water. Pour over the aubergines. Bake at 350°F/180°C/Gas Mark 4 for 1 hour.

Orange Beef Fritter Cakes

	Imperial	*Metric*	*American*
Flour	*4 oz*	*100 g*	*1 cup*
Salt and pepper			
Egg	*1*	*1*	*1*
Milk	*½ pint*	*250 ml*	*1¼ cups*
Pinch of chives			
Raw minced beef	*1 lb*	*450 g*	*2 cups*
Onion, large	*1*	*1*	*1*
Fat or oil for frying			
Bunch of watercress	*1*	*1*	*1*
Orange	*1*	*1*	*1*

Sieve flour, salt and pepper into a bowl. Gradually mix in beaten egg and milk to make a smooth batter and add the chives. Stir beef and chopped onion into the batter and leave for 30 minutes. Slowly heat oil $\frac{1}{4}$ in. deep in a frying pan. Spoon rounded tablespoons of the mixture into hot fat. Lower heat and fry cakes for 5 minutes, turning from time to time, until batter is crisp and the meat is cooked. Garnish with watercress and slices of peeled orange.

Serve with a green salad and an onion salad.
Drink beer or cider.
Follow with a slice of cream gâteau.

Tiered Pancakes

	Imperial	Metric	American
Milk	½ pint	250 ml	1¼ cups
Egg	1	1	1
Flour	2 oz	50 g	½ cup
Cooked minced beef	4 oz	100 g	¾ cup
Salt and pepper			
Cheddar cheese, grated	8 oz	200 g	½ lb
Tomatoes	8 oz	200 g	½ lb

Mix milk, egg and flour smoothly and leave to stand for 1 hour. Cook thin pancakes with the batter, spread with hot seasoned beef and tomato slices and build up layer by layer until all mixture is used. Keep the pile of pancakes in a warm oven. Top with the grated cheese and place under the grill, until cheese is brown and bubbling. Serve hot, cut into wedges.

Beefy Cheese Peppers

	Imperial	Metric	American
Green peppers, large	4	4	4
Bread, crumbled	6 oz	150 g	4 cups
Milk	4 tbsp	4 tbsp	4 tbsp
Parsley, chopped	½ tbsp	½ tbsp	½ tbsp
Salt and pepper			
Tomato chutney	2 tbsp	2 tbsp	2 tbsp
Soft cheese	2 oz	50 g	¼ cup
Cooked minced beef	2 oz	50 g	⅜ cup

Cut off the tops of the peppers, scoop out cores and seeds and wash carefully. Drop the peppers into boiling water, and cook for 3 minutes. Crumble the bread and soak in the milk. Mix in parsley, tomato chutney, cheese and beef. Fill the peppers with this mixture, and replace the tops. Put in a baking tin with a little water. Bake at 400°F/200°C/Gas Mark 6 for 30 minutes until tender. Serve with hot tomato sauce.

Stuffed Aubergines

	Imperial	*Metric*	*American*
Aubergines, medium	*2*	*2*	*2*
Pinch of salt			
Olive oil	*2 tsp*	*2 tsp*	*2 tsp*
Raw minced beef	*2 oz*	*50 g*	*¼ cup*
Parsley, chopped	*½ tbsp*	*½ tbsp*	*½ tbsp*
Tomato	*1*	*1*	*1*
Breadcrumbs	*2 oz*	*50 g*	*½ cup*
Cheddar cheese, grated	*5 oz*	*125 g*	*1⅞ cups*
Onion, small	*1*	*1*	*1*

Wash the aubergines, remove the stalks and cut in half lengthwise, and scoop out core and seeds. Lightly score the surface of each half aubergine to ensure even cooking. Sprinkle with salt and olive oil, and bake at 400°F/200°C/Gas Mark 6 for 15 minutes until the centre is almost cooked. Chop the tomato and onion, and grate the cheese. Make stuffing by mixing all the remaining ingredients together, reserving 1 oz/25 g cheese. Scoop out half the aubergine flesh, chop up and add to stuffing. Fill the aubergine cases with the mixture, top with the remaining grated cheese, and return to the oven for 15 minutes. Courgettes may be used instead of aubergines.

Serve on a bed of boiled rice.
Drink beer or cider.
Follow with apples stewed in cider with raisins.

Baked Stuffed Onions

	Imperial	Metric	American
Onion, large	*4*	*4*	*4*
Streaky bacon rashers	*2*	*2*	*2*
Raw minced beef	*12 oz*	*300 g*	*1½ cups*
Flour	*1½ oz*	*40 g*	*¼ cup+ 2 tbsp*
Salt and pepper			
Pinch of marjoram			
Garlic clove	*½–1*	*½–1*	*½–1*
Beef stock	*½ pint*	*250 ml*	*1¼ cups*
Cooking apple	*1*	*1*	*1*
Tomatoes, small can	*1*	*1*	*1*

Peel onions, leaving them whole and with the root end intact. Place in a large saucepan, cover with cold water and bring to the boil. Lower the heat, cover with a lid and cook for 40 minutes. Remove rind and bone from the bacon, and cut the bacon into small pieces, add minced beef and fry for about 4 minutes, stirring occasionally, until browned. Stir in the flour and seasonings and crushed garlic and cook for 2 minutes. Add the stock to the pan and bring to the boil, stirring well. Peel the apple and grate into the mince mixture. Reduce the heat, cover and simmer for 15 minutes. Drain the onions, cut across the top of each and scoop out the insides. Place the onions in a shallow, ovenware dish and fill each onion with mince mixture. Mix the remainder of the beef with the tomatoes. Season to taste and pour around the onions. Cover with foil and bake at 375°F/190°C/Gas Mark 5 for 45 minutes.

Serve with some creamy mashed potatoes.

Garlic Mince Balls

	Imperial	*Metric*	*American*
Raw minced beef	*1 lb*	*450 g*	*2 cups*
Salt and pepper			
Onion, medium	*1*	*1*	*1*
Garlic clove	½	½	½
Butter or margarine	*3 oz*	*75 g*	*⅜ cup*
Breadcrumbs	*2 oz*	*50 g*	*½ cup*
Milk	*4 tbsp*	*4 tbsp*	*4 tbsp*
Flour	*1 oz*	*25 g*	*¼ cup*
Stock	*¾ pint*	*375 ml*	*1⅞ cups*

Mix meat with salt and pepper. Chop the onion and fry it in 1 oz/25 g butter for a few minutes and blend with meat. Soften the breadcrumbs in milk, then stir into meat mixture. Mix well, add crushed garlic and form into 18 small balls. Heat the rest of the butter or margarine in a large, shallow pan. Coat the balls in seasoned flour and fry until golden brown. Add the stock and simmer gently for 15 minutes.

Serve with creamy mashed potatoes, peas or beans.
Drink red wine or beer.
Follow with a chocolate cream gâteau.

Layer Pie with Yogurt Topping

	Imperial	*Metric*	*American*
Onion	*4 oz*	*100 g*	*¼ lb*
Butter	*1 oz*	*25 g*	*⅛ cup*
Cooked minced beef	*8 oz*	*200 g*	*1½ cups*
Pinch of mixed herbs			
Tomato purée	*2 tbsp*	*2 tbsp*	*2 tbsp*
Worcestershire sauce	*1 tsp*	*1 tsp*	*1 tsp*
Salt and pepper			
Sliced cooked potatoes	*1 lb*	*450 g*	*1 lb*
Tomatoes	*8 oz*	*200 g*	*½ lb*
Egg	*1*	*1*	*1*
Flour	*1 oz*	*25 g*	*¼ cup*
Natural yoghurt	*¼ pint*	*125 ml*	*⅝ cup*
Parsley, chopped			
Paprika			

Cook the chopped onions in butter. Add the cooked minced beef, mixed herbs, tomato purée and Worcestershire sauce, salt and pepper. Arrange alternate layers of meat and potato finishing with potato. Cover the casserole and bake at 375°F/190°C/Gas Mark 5 for 30 minutes. Beat egg and add flour, yogurt and parsley. Pour over the pie, and bake for a further 20 minutes. Sprinkle top with paprika before serving.

Serve with carrots, peas or beans.

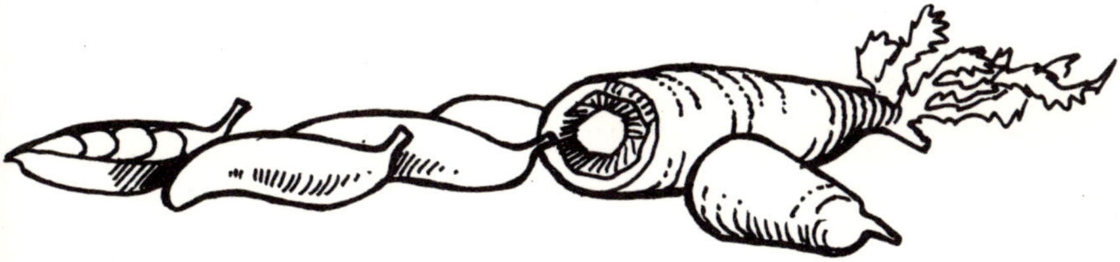

Beef and Rice Dish

	Imperial	*Metric*	*American*
Patna rice	*8 oz*	*200 g*	*1¼ cups*
Onions	*8 oz*	*200 g*	*½ lb*
Butter	*4 oz*	*100 g*	*½ cup*
Raw minced beef	*10 oz*	*250 g*	*1¼ cups*
Mixed vegetables, cooked or frozen	*10 oz*	*250 g*	*1½ cups*
Soy sauce	*2 tbsp*	*2 tbsp*	*2 tbsp*
Curry powder	*1 tsp*	*1 tsp*	*1 tsp*
Salt and pepper			
Tomatoes	*2*	*2*	*2*

A thin one-egg omelette, fried flat like a pancake and turned

Cook the rice in boiling, salted water for 12 minutes. Turn into a sieve and separate rice grains by rinsing with cold, running water until the surplus starch is removed. Allow to drain. Slice the onions and fry in 2 oz/50 g butter in a large pan with the meat. Brown slowly for 20 minutes over medium heat. Add the remaining butter, rice, mixed vegetables, pepper and salt, curry powder and soy sauce. Blend well over medium heat until very hot. Turn into an ovenware dish, and garnish with strips of omelette. Decorate with tomato wedges around the edge of the dish. Place under grill for a few seconds and serve with green salad.

Serve with chutney or dill pickles.
Drink lager or cider.
Follow with fresh fruit salad and cream.

Nutty Beef Roll

	Imperial	*Metric*	*American*
Pastry			
Self-raising flour or flour sifted with 2 tsp baking powder	*7 oz*	*200 g*	*1¾ cups*
Pinch of salt			
Suet, shredded	*4 oz*	*100 g*	*½ cup*
Pinch of caraway seeds			
Cold water to mix			
Filling			
Raw minced beef	*1 lb*	*450 g*	*2 cups*
Oil	*1 tbsp*	*1 tbsp*	*1 tbsp*
Onion, small	*1*	*1*	*1*
Mango chutney	*3 tbsp*	*3 tbsp*	*3 tbsp*
Walnuts	*2 oz*	*50 g*	*½ cup*
Fresh white breadcrumbs	*1 oz*	*25 g*	*⅔ cup*

Sieve the flour and salt into a bowl and add suet and caraway seeds. Add enough cold water to give a soft, manageable dough. Roll out on a floured surface to about 11 in. by 13 in. (28 cm by 33 cm). Fry the mince in the oil with the chopped onion for 5 minutes. Stir in the remaining ingredients and spread over the pastry to within ½ in./1 cm of the edges. Roll up the pastry, starting from one short side, and finishing with the seam underneath. Pinch the ends to seal and wrap loosely in greased foil. Place on a baking sheet. Bake at 325°F/170°C/Gas Mark 3 for 1 hour. Serve in thick slices with a rich brown onion gravy.

Jacket potatoes can go in the oven at the same time.

Spiced Beef with Aubergines

	Imperial	Metric	American
Raw minced beef	2 lb	1 kg	4 cups
Lard	1 oz	25 g	1/8 cup
Onion	8 oz	200 g	1/2 lb
Turmeric	1 tsp	1 tsp	1 tsp
Chili seasoning	1 tsp	1 tsp	1 tsp
Ground cumin	1 tsp	1 tsp	1 tsp
Salt	1 tsp	1 tsp	1 tsp
Curry paste	2 tbsp	2 tbsp	2 tbsp
Mango chutney	3 tbsp	3 tbsp	3 tbsp
Sultanas	3 oz	75 g	3/4 cup
Margarine	1 oz	25 g	1/8 cup
Worcestershire sauce	1 tbsp	1 tbsp	1 tbsp
Beef stock	1/2 pint	250 ml	1 1/4 cups
Aubergines	1 lb	450 g	1 lb

Fry the mince in the lard to seal. Add the chopped onion, turmeric, chili, cumin, salt and curry paste and cook for 5 minutes, stirring well. Add the chutney, sultanas, margarine, Worcestershire sauce and stock. Bring to the boil, reduce heat and simmer for 1 hour. Slice the aubergines and sprinkle with salt and leave for 5 minutes. Rinse and dry thoroughly and add to the pan. Simmer gently for 30 minutes. Serve with boiled rice.

Serve with a variety of chutneys and some thinly sliced cucumber in yogurt.
Drink lager or cider.
Follow with ice cream or fresh fruit salad.

Minced Beef with Creamed Peppers

	Imperial	*Metric*	*American*
Butter	*2 oz*	*50 g*	*1/4 cup*
Onion	*4 oz*	*100 g*	*1/4 lb*
Green pepper	*1*	*1*	*1*
Red pepper	*1*	*1*	*1*
Raw minced beef	*1 lb*	*450 g*	*2 cups*
Button mushrooms	*8 oz*	*200 g*	*1/2 lb*
Beef stock	*1/4 pint*	*125 ml*	*5/8 cup*
Flour	*1 1/2 oz*	*40 g*	*1/4 cup+ 2 tbsp*
Milk	*1/4 pint*	*125 ml*	*5/8 cup*
Salt and pepper			
Soured cream	*1/4 pint*	*125 ml*	*5/8 cup*
Parsley, chopped			
Mixed herbs			

Melt half the butter and gently fry the chopped onions and peppers for 5 minutes. Add the mince and mushrooms and cook for 5 minutes stirring well. Add the stock, cover and simmer for 30 minutes. Drain liquid from meat and reserve. Melt the remaining butter, stir in flour and cook for 2 minutes. Gradually add the liquid from the meat, together with the milk. Cook gently, stirring, until the sauce thickens. Add the meat and vegetables to the sauce, bring to the boil and adjust seasoning to taste. Turn into a warmed serving dish, swirl in the soured cream and sprinkle with parsley and mixed herbs.

Beefburgers in Wine Sauce

	Imperial	*Metric*	*American*
Raw minced beef	*12 oz*	*300 g*	*1½ cups*
Onion, small	*1*	*1*	*1*
Fresh white breadcrumbs	*2 oz*	*50 g*	*1⅓ cups*
Parsley, chopped	*1 tbsp*	*1 tbsp*	*1 tbsp*
Egg	*1*	*1*	*1*
Salt and pepper			
Oil or lard for frying			
Red Wine Cook-in-sauce, 13½ oz/375 g can	*1*	*1*	*1*
Watercress to garnish			

Combine the mince, chopped onion, breadcrumbs, parsley, egg, salt and pepper in a bowl. Divide into eight round shapes. Fry in hot fat until brown, turning once. Drain off any excess fat. Pour the red wine sauce into the pan. Bring to the boil, then reduce heat, cover and simmer for 30 minutes, stirring occasionally. Garnish with watercress.

Serve with creamy mashed potatoes and a green salad. Drink red wine.
Follow with a cream gâteau, or with fresh fruit salad topped with liqueur-flavoured whipped cream and small sweet biscuits.

Beef Gougere

	Imperial	*Metric*	*American*
Butter	*2½ oz*	*65 g*	*¼ cup+ 1 tbsp*
Water	*¼ pint*	*125 ml*	*⅝ cup*
Flour	*4 oz*	*100 g*	*1 cup*
Eggs	*2*	*2*	*2*
Milk	*3 tbsp*	*3 tbsp*	*3 tbsp*
Cheddar cheese, grated	*6 oz*	*150 g*	*2¼ cups*
Onion	*1*	*1*	*1*
Cooked minced beef	*2 oz*	*50 g*	*⅜ cup*
Salt and pepper			

Place 1½ oz/40 g/3 tbsp butter and water in a saucepan. Bring to the boil, then add 2½ oz/ 65 g/⅝ cup flour. Beat mixture until it forms a ball leaving the sides of the saucepan clear. Beat eggs one at a time into the mixture. Grease a round, shallow ovenware dish. Spoon mixture around the sides of the dish leaving a space in the centre. Place remaining butter, flour and milk in saucepan and heat stirring until sauce thickens. Add cheese, chopped onion and beef and mix well. Pour into the centre of the prepared dish. Bake at 400°F/200°C/ Gas Mark 6 until well risen and golden brown. Serve hot, garnish with watercress or parsley.
Peas or beans go well with this.

Hot Beef Party Savouries

	Imperial	*Metric*	*American*
Butter	*½ oz*	*12 g*	*1 tbsp*
Flour	*1 oz*	*25 g*	*⅛ cup*
Chicken stock	*¾ pint*	*375 ml*	*1⅞ cups*
Mayonnaise	*2 fl. oz*	*50 ml*	*¼ cup*
Mushrooms	*1 oz*	*25 g*	*⅜ cup*
Cooked minced beef	*1 lb*	*450 g*	*3 cups*
Cream	*2 fl. oz*	*50 ml*	*¼ cup*
Parsley, chopped	*½ tbsp*	*½ tbsp*	*½ tbsp*
Mixed herbs	*½ tbsp*	*½ tbsp*	*½ tbsp*
Seasoned flour			
Oil for deep frying			
Salt and pepper			

In a saucepan heat the butter, add the flour, mix well and cook for 1 minute. Remove from the heat, add chicken stock and then cook, stirring continuously until the sauce thickens. Slice and cook the mushrooms in a frying pan. Add the beef, and mayonnaise, cream, parsley and herbs and season to taste. Mix the ingredients well, and put the mixture into the refrigerator until firm. Make into small balls and roll in seasoned flour. Fry in hot deep oil until brown and drain on kitchen paper.

Serve with a big bowl of chutney to dip the beef balls in.
Serve with red or white wine or beer.
Follow with slices of fresh pineapple sprinkled with sugar and coconut.

Index